Sask**Scandal**

*Sask***Scandal**

THE DEATH OF POLITICAL IDEALISM IN SASKATCHEWAN

Gerry Jones

FIFTH
HOUSE

Front cover photograph by John Perret

Design by Articulate Eye

The publisher gratefully acknowledges the support of The Canada Council for the Arts and the Department of Canadian Heritage.

THE CANADA COUNCIL | LE CONSEIL DES ARTS
FOR THE ARTS | DU CANADA
SINCE 1957 | DEPUIS 1957

We acknowledge the financial support of the Government of Canada through the Book Publishing Industry Development Program for our publishing activities.

Printed in Canada.

00 01 02 03 04/ 5 4 3 2 1

CANADIAN CATALOGUING IN PUBLICATION DATA

Jones, Gerry, 1945–
    Saskscandal
    ISBN 1-894004-58-2
    1. Saskatchewan—Politics and government—1982-1991.*
I. Title.
FC3527.2.J66 2000   971.24'03   C00-911160-3   FC1071.J66 2000

Published in Canada by

Fifth House Ltd.
A Fitzhenry & Whiteside Company
1511-1800 4 Street SW
Calgary, Alberta, Canada
T2S 2S5

Table of Contents

Trouble Brewing   1

The Whistleblower   11

The Police Investigation   20

Caucus Captain Sinks with the Ship   38

The Saddle and the Kickback   54

The Tory Walls Come Tumbling Down   62

The Courthouse Parade   72

A Cold Tory Winter   90

Michael Hopfner's Soap   102

John Gerich Tries a Jury   127

Sherwin Petersen's Forensic Team   136

The Courthouse Parade Continues   148

The Senator's Judgement Day   156

The Tory Casket   179

Appendix: Summary of Cases in Project Fiddle   189

Trouble Brewing

In the early fall of 1991, the Saskatchewan Progressive Conservative Party was preparing to go to the voters for the second time after nine uninterrupted years of Tory government. Its leader was Grant Devine, a short man with the gift of the gab and a flare for theatrics whose goal while in power was to keep government at arm's length from private enterprise. "I can tolerate a lot of government in health and education," he used to say, "but I can't tolerate government running farms or building new businesses, pumping oil, mining, or in the forestry business." In the heady days of the early 1980s, when Devine's term began, he considered himself Saskatchewan's number-one salesperson, the man who would bring wealth to his province. His sales pitches, at home and abroad, were peppered with folksy sayings, such as "There's so much more we can be," "Give 'er snooze, Bruce," and "Don't say whoa in a mud hole."

Devine's business-oriented approach and down-home style helped give the Tories a landslide victory over the incumbent New Democrats in the 1982 provincial election, and had allowed them to squeak by in 1986. By 1991, however, the Tories knew they were in trouble. The government had failed to deliver on its promise of wealth for the people, and while Devine was out in the country trying to bolster the party's sagging fortunes, back in the provincial capital a storm was brewing that would eventually destroy his party.

Early in the 1991 election campaign, RCMP officers paid an unexpected call on the Tory caucus office at the Saskatchewan Legislature. Shortly thereafter, the panicked caucus communications director, John Scraba, called on the chair of the Tory re-election campaign, Senator Eric Berntson. This much is clear.

There are conflicting reports about what happened next.

In later court testimony, Eric Berntson confirmed that John Scraba arrived at the Tory campaign headquarters to tell him that the RCMP had come to the caucus office looking for financial records. Berntson said he found this alarming because, as campaign chair, he had no desire to see irregularities in the caucus office blow up in the election campaign. He said Scraba reassured him, telling him the records had been destroyed. "This investigation stops with me," Scraba stated. Berntson then said Scraba suggested that if Berntson told the RCMP that what the caucus was doing was okay, perhaps the problem would go away. He also claimed that Scraba announced, "If I'm going down, I'm going to be taking a lot of people with me." At the time of his testimony, Berntson called Scraba's comments "the desperation of a desperate man." He commented, "I didn't feel terribly threatened personally, but I felt the organization I had put blood, sweat, and tears in for the last ten years was in serious danger of disintegrating because of this potential scandal."

John Scraba's recollection of their meeting was somewhat different. While he admitted to the conversation with Berntson at the PC Party's campaign headquarters, he said he did not suggest to Berntson that anyone tell the police to back off, nor did he threaten to take others with him if he went down. Grant Devine, for his part, said he learned of the investigation into caucus finances while he was out touring the province and talking to voters. He said he asked his principal secretary, John Weir, to find out what was going on while he tried to focus on the election campaign.

Out in the field, Devine had his work cut out for him. Saskatchewan voters, it seemed, were tiring of their experiment with Tory politics. The roots of the Saskatchewan Conservative Party had been planted beneath the endless prairie sky in 1903, when a group of Conservatives from the region had formed the Conservative Association. Apart from a brief stint in a coalition government in 1929, the Conservatives were basically shut out of the Saskatchewan Legislature until 1964, when they won a single seat. Eleven years later, in 1975, the Tories took seven seats. Three years later, they replaced the Liberals as the official opposition with seventeen seats to the NDP's forty-four. Then on April 26, 1982, under their new leader Grant Devine, the Conservatives won a landslide victory, taking fifty-five seats, the largest legislative majority in Saskatchewan history. The New Democrats tumbled from forty-four MLAs to nine.

The track record of the NDP and its predecessor, the CCF (the Co-operative Commonwealth Federation), had been one of political innovation for the public good. The tough climate and co-operative, pioneering spirit of the Canadian prairies had forged a brand of politics that gave rise to Medicare, and one of the most important legacies of years of socialist rule was the province's Crown corporations. For Tommy Douglas, the CCF premier elected in 1944, Crown corporations were the policy instruments that would overcome the failure of the marketplace to meet the needs of Saskatchewan residents. The province's first Crowns, most of them utilities such as SaskTel, SaskPower, and Saskatchewan Government Insurance, were established in the 1940s. The second phase of Crowns came in the 1970s when NDP Premier Allan Blakeney came to power. Blakeney felt that the Saskatchewan people were not receiving their fair share from oil, potash, and other minerals, so he and his team used the Crowns to develop the province's natural resources. The new Crowns included SaskOil, the Potash Corporation of Saskatchewan, and the Saskatchewan Mining Development Corporation. Under the NDP, the Crowns had four main goals: to strengthen and diversify the economy; to create jobs and promote regional development; to provide a vehicle for Saskatchewan's control over its economy; and to improve government programs and services with the money they earned.

As Blakeney expanded the province's Crown corporations, especially those dealing with resources such as potash and uranium, voters began to complain that he appeared to be more interested in building industries than in promoting social issues, the traditional mainstay of the New Democrats. There were also claims that he was preoccupied with federal constitutional negotiations and was not paying enough attention to the people back home. These criticisms of NDP policy were compounded by western disenchantment with Liberal Prime Minister Pierre Trudeau. This led Saskatchewan Liberals to move in droves to the provincial Conservative Party. By early 1982, with Grant Devine at the helm, the Conservatives emerged as the real alternative to the NDP.

Allan Blakeney decided to test his party at the polls on April 26, 1982, even though he didn't have to call an election until October of the following year. His advisors felt it was better to go sooner rather than later because the Canadian economy was heading into a recession, and the political prospects for incumbent governments were likely to get worse rather than better. The New Democrats' campaign ran into trouble even before it was officially launched.

The day before the election was announced, the government legislated five thousand non-medical hospital workers back to work, ending a sixteen-day legal strike. Unions, the New Democrats' traditional allies, were angry. Union leaders argued that the two sides were close to a negotiated settlement and accused the government of acting too hastily. Allan Blakeney disagreed, suggesting that the Canadian Union of Public Employees, the union that represented the strikers, was planning to escalate the strike. The government's back-to-work legislation also prohibited strikes in all essential services for the duration of the election campaign. Union protesters dogged the premier throughout the campaign.

Labour unrest wasn't the only issue the NDP had to struggle with. The Tories and the Liberals were criticizing the New Democrats' pre-election budget, and it wasn't going over well on the streets either. The budget was balanced, as the previous eleven budgets had been. There was money for health care, education, and social programs, but there was no tax relief for middle-income people. The Tories had done their homework. According to the pollsters they had hired, voters were worried about inflation, interest rates, and high taxes. With their so-called pocketbook campaign, the Tories offered Saskatchewan voters substantial tax cuts and a mortgage-interest-reduction plan to help homeowners struggling with an 18-percent interest rate.

Grant Devine's troops were counting on victory and as election day approached, they became more confident. In Devine's riding of Estevan, his election team booked a basement room at a local hotel for the anticipated victory party. As election day drew near, they realized the room would be too small, so they moved to the Estevan Curling Club. When the ballots were counted, the cheers of the seven hundred people in the curling club spread out like a fresh breeze rippling the prairie grasses.

"This is fantastic," Devine told the boisterous crowd. "I expected somewhere between thirty-five and forty seats," he later told reporters. "But this is incredible." Grant Devine and his team, most of them new gladiators in the political arena, now had the government and the political power in Saskatchewan.

The new premier of the province was born July 4, 1944, in Regina. He was raised on a farm that his grandfather had homesteaded near Lake Valley, not far from Moose Jaw, and attended school locally. After high school, he earned a Bachelor of Science degree in agriculture from the University of Saskatchewan in Saskatoon. After a stint as a marketing specialist with the Department of Agriculture in Ottawa, he returned to the West and earned two master's degrees at the University of Alberta, one in agricultural economics and the other in business administration. Then, after receiving a PhD in agricultural economics from Ohio State University in 1976, he accepted a position at the University of Saskatchewan, where he taught courses in consumer economics and agricultural marketing. He ran as a Tory in a Saskatoon riding in the 1978 general election. He was soundly defeated but far from ready to give up on politics. The following year he entered the race for the leadership of the Saskatchewan Conservative Party. A flashy campaign, complete with a brass band and balloons, won him the leadership on the first ballot at the November 1979 leadership convention.

Devine appointed as his deputy Eric Berntson, the man who has often been credited with recruiting Grant Devine into politics and the Tory Party in 1978. Berntson was first elected as a member of the Legislative Assembly in the traditionally Conservative rural riding of Souris-Cannington in 1975. He was appointed minister of agriculture and government house leader in the new government's first cabinet. Some Conservatives say Berntson soon became the administrative head of the government handling day-to-day decision-making, while Grant Devine became the front man waving the Tory flag and carrying the message throughout the land.

When Devine swept to power in 1982, one of his avowed goals was to greatly reduce the number of Crown corporations in the province. Up to then, the Potash Corporation of Saskatchewan had been the only resource Crown to pay significant dividends. The New Democrats viewed the resource Crowns as long-term investments. They often bragged about the social contribution the Crowns provided—about twelve thousand jobs and spin-offs for Saskatchewan companies. The New Democrats kept a tight rein on the Crown corporations to ensure they followed their mandate. Cabinet ministers served as chairs of the Crowns and many of their top executives came up through the civil service. The Tories, on the other hand, blamed the Crowns for any difficulties with the provincial economy. They argued that the corporations were full of incompetent managers and were a drain on the provincial treasury. They also alleged that the management structure allowed for too much political interference in how the companies were run. A year after it grabbed power from the NDP, the Devine government took control of the Crowns by appointing well-known Tory supporters as chairs of Crown boards. The road to privatization had been opened, but it was slow going because the Crowns still held a special place in the lives of many people in Saskatchewan, including many people who had voted for the Conservatives.

When the Tories took over Saskatchewan, Devine declared the province "open for business," and he hit the road trying to drum up new corporate offices for the breadbasket of the country. Some of the ventures that responded to this call were less successful than others. Take, for example, Char Incorporated, a barbecue briquette plant set up by a Quebec businessman in Grant Devine's own riding of Estevan. The provincial government provided a $220,000 loan from the Saskatchewan Economic Development Corporation. The province put in an additional $145,000 and the federal Department of Regional Economic

Expansion contributed a grant of $182,413. The business closed after only three weeks and laid off all but three employees, who remained to make kitty litter. Or consider Supercart International, a company that was to open a plant in Regina to manufacture plastic shopping carts. A few prototypes were produced, but that was it. Before it declared bankruptcy, the company had received $366,000 from the federal government, $250,000 from the provincial government, $400,000 from the Saskatchewan Economic Development Corporation, $65,000 from the City of Regina, and $1 million through the provincial Venture Capital Corporation.

Like many provincial governments of the day, the Saskatchewan Conservatives were hooked on high-tech. That led to a couple of extravagant mistakes. Joytec was going to build computerized golf simulators in the province. It received nearly $1.3 million in tax credits and a $76,000 provincial grant. Then a Vancouver-based financier bought out Joytec, and the company was moved to British Columbia, taking the Saskatchewan government's investment with it. Another case was GigaText Translation Services, which received $5.25 million in government investment and loans to produce perfect English-to-French translation by computer. No translations ever took place, and the only money recovered was when the assets were auctioned off and a local computer company picked up the computers and furniture.

Near the end of Grand Devine's first term in office, trouble was looming on the prairie horizon. Oil prices had collapsed, potash prices were down, and the uranium market was struggling. On top of that, the agriculture sector was in deep trouble as world wheat prices fell in wheat subsidy wars. A third of Saskatchewan's farmers were on the edge of bankruptcy. In the midst of this, support for the Conservatives slipped badly.

In the 1986 election campaign, the Devine government decided to concentrate on rural Saskatchewan, its natural constituency. Although support for the Tories was weak in urban centres (especially the major cities of Regina and Saskatoon), the Tory rural base appeared to be intact, despite the farm crisis and some Liberal incursions. Just to be on the safe side, however, Grant Devine took over the agriculture portfolio. Prior to spring seeding in 1986, the provincial government offered farmers a $25 per acre low-interest farm production loan. The loan was available to all farmers, even those who didn't need it. There were also cash advances and tax credits for livestock producers. The Farmers' Oil Royalty Refund was implemented to give each producer an average rebate of $650. Devine continued to lobby the federal Conservative government for more farm aid. In the final days of the 1986 election campaign, Brian Mulroney's Conservative government came through with a promise of $1 billion for a special Canadian grains payment. Conservative support began to recover from its low point in late 1985, and in early 1986, there was talk of an election. On October 20, 1986, the people of Saskatchewan went to the polls.

On election day, more people voted for the NDP (45.06 percent) than for the PCs (44.80 percent), but the Tories captured more seats (thirty-eight compared with twenty-five for the NDP). The Liberals had 9.92 percent, up from 4.5 percent in 1982, and elected one member. The New Democrats got the majority vote, but the Tories got the government.

The NDP took twenty of twenty-four seats in the larger urban centres of Regina and Saskatoon. The Tories won seven of eight seats in the smaller urban centres such as Melfort, Melville, Swift Current, and Yorkton, and all but three of the thirty rural seats. The two seats in the northern part of the province went to the NDP.

Back on the political throne, the Tories soon faced more trouble. In the late 1980s, as the province's debt and deficit climbed, the Conservatives cut social programs and raised taxes. There were also cuts in government grants for education, legal aid, and the prescription drug program. The children's dental plan was scrapped. Amongst the socialist left, the late 1980s became known as "the years of the cutting knives."

On the business side, the Conservatives' private enterprise bus continued to roll along and even began to pick up a bit of speed. In 1987 Grant Devine announced the death of socialism and the privatization of all Crown corporations except the utilities, and a department of public participation was established to push through the government's privatization plans. Throughout 1988 and 1989, a large number of public holdings were privatized, including a sodium sulphate mine, a peat moss operation, a printing company, a forest products company, pieces of SaskTel, and uranium and potash assets.

The government's privatization moves stirred strong emotions on the political left. When the Tories moved to put the natural gas company SaskEnergy up for sale, the NDP walked out of the Legislative Assembly, and the Provincial Legislature ground to a halt for seventeen days. The NDP returned only after Devine agreed to let the natural gas bill die on the order paper. After this confrontation, Devine shuffled his cabinet and decided to "re-examine" his privatization strategy, although that didn't stop him from proceeding with the sale of the Potash Corporation of Saskatchewan (PCS). That sale didn't prompt much of an outcry though, mainly because PCS wasn't a utility like SaskEnergy.

By the late 1980s, Grant Devine was beginning to take a lot of heat. With the storm over privatization brewing in the background and the provincial debt growing, the Tory team had to turn its thoughts to another provincial election. NDP support was increasing and the Liberals were holding ground, especially in rural Saskatchewan. As a last-ditch effort to shore up the farm vote, Devine announced the harmonization of the provincial sales tax with the federal Goods and Services Tax (GST). The extra money that would be raised by extending the provincial sales tax into many new areas, such as restaurant meals, would go to farm safety nets, such as the Gross Revenue Insurance Program and the Net Income Stabilization Account. The government estimated harmonization would provide an extra $105 million in the first year and $150 million in each subsequent year to help farmers. The NDP promised to scrap harmonization as soon as it was elected.

Then in one more last-ditch effort to woo rural voters, Grant Devine announced the Fair Share Program. The Conservatives promised to decentralize government services and to move up to two thousand jobs from Regina to rural areas. Not only did the plan not go over well with many voters, but it also caused trouble within Tory ranks. Grant Hodgins, a young, sharp-witted cabinet minister who had often been mentioned as a natural successor to Devine, abruptly resigned on June 17, 1991. He announced his resignation dramatically in the Legislative Assembly without having informed the premier. A rattled Devine prorogued the Legislature, despite the fact that the budget and a raft of proposed bills had not been passed.

The Conservatives hung onto power to the bitter end hoping things would turn around. A provincial election was held on October 21, 1991. The New Democrats took fifty-five seats, the Tories took ten, and the Liberals took one. Prior to the Tories taking over in 1982, Saskatchewan had gone through a string of balanced or surplus budgets in thirty-six of thirty-eight years. That included CCF, Liberal, and NDP governments. When the New Democrats looked at the provincial books after the 1991 election, they found that the public debt stood at around $15 billion, about $15,000 for every man, woman, and child in Saskatchewan, the worst provincial debt load in Canada. Dismissed to the opposition side of the Legislature by the voters after their free-spending years in power, the Tories soon discovered that their nightmare had only just begun.

The Whistleblower

As Grant Devine and his colleagues were licking their wounds after their slamming political defeat, things went from bad to worse in Regina when the Royal Canadian Mounted Police moved in on the PC caucus office. The trouble had begun that spring.

In early May 1991, across the Saskatchewan prairie, farmers were getting their tractors ready for the fields. In Regina, the elm trees that tower up from sidewalks in the downtown were in bud. Along the sides of office towers, the first blades of grass were pushing through the leaves left over from the fall. It was spring, the season of change. But there was more change in the wind than anyone could have imagined, and it all began with a conversation in a hotel lounge.

Three people huddled over their drinks at the Regina Inn as they talked in hushed voices. Paul Raphael de Montigny, an employee of the Crown utility SaskPower, was disturbed by what he was hearing. With him were his wife and Marilyn Borowski, the head of Financial Services in the Legislative Assembly. Borowski was doing most of the talking. Two months later, on July 5, de Montigny sat down with an RCMP officer whom he had summoned to his home. De Montigny gave the officer a statement about his conversation with Borowski, the gist of which was that there appeared to be some shady financial dealings going on at the PC caucus office.

The seeds of wrongdoing had been planted nine years earlier, the day after the April 1982 election when the Tories had whipped the New Democrats. That day money, lots of it, had started to flow into the Tory caucus office in the form of Caucus Sessional Research Grants and the Secretarial Grants paid out to the caucus office by the Financial Services department of the Legislative Assembly. These grants were calculated according to the number of elected members, and they were intended to cover the costs of administrative, research, and secretarial support for the MLAs. The grants were paid out on the honour system and caucuses were not required to report back to the Legislature on how the money was spent.

As the Tories had won fifty-five seats in the 1982 election, the payoff in MLA grants that year was considerable. Although the money was supposed to be used so the caucus office could provide office and research support to its MLAs, in practice the caucus could spend the money in any way it felt most benefitted the party. Indeed, many MLAs viewed it as money that, instead of being used to support the current administration, could be put toward ensuring success in the next election. According to one former MLA, in 1982 the Conservatives had so much money pouring in that they couldn't spend it fast enough.

By late 1985, near the end of the Conservatives' first term in office, the caucus bank account was flush with cash. A plan known only to an initiated few was devised to clean out the caucus account and stash most of the money—$450,000—in a secret bank account in Martensville, a small town north of Saskatoon. The money was to be used for the election that had to be called the following year. Ralph Katzman, a veteran MLA and loyal soldier, was chosen to handle the cash. A former MLA said he was told it wasn't the first time that the caucus account had been cleaned out. There is no way to check out this statement however, because back in the 1980s, caucus accounts were not audited and caucus records were destroyed at the end of each year to keep them out of enemy hands.

When this money became an issue in the 1990s, Ralph Katzman was interviewed by the Regina *Leader-Post*. In the June 1995 interview, Katzman told a reporter that the caucus was under no obligation to disclose how it spent its grants. "One question [in the Board of Internal Economy, the body that set the rules for MLA grants and allowances] was, if a guy wanted to stand on the top of the Bessborough [hotel in Saskatoon] and throw away $20 bills, did the grant say you can't do that?"

Katzman had once sat on the Board of Internal Economy. "Everybody on the committee laughed and said, 'No, you spend a grant the way you think it will do you the best good.'"

This steady stream of money in the form of loosely regulated caucus grants may have been what set the tone for later dealings in the Tory caucus office, but it was not information about the caucus grant money that brought de Montigny to the RCMP. The big catch from de Montigny's information, the one that would land a lot of Tories in the frying pan, concerned the MLAs' Communication Allowances. It came from a plan spawned in Cypress Hills Provincial Park, in the southwest corner of the province, early in the Conservatives' second term in office.

A Communication Allowance is the money each MLA is entitled to collect to pay for expenses he or she incurs when communicating with constituents. In the late 1980s, the amount each member was entitled to collect was calculated by multiplying the cost of mailing four first-class letters by the number of registered voters in the MLA's constituency. When the Tories were in power, the average amount available to an MLA was approximately $13,000 a year. There was no requirement that a member spend all of the allowance, and any money not spent by the end of the year was lost.

The members' handbook, which was given to each MLA when he or she was first elected, contained the regulations governing Communication Allowances and a list of eligible and ineligible expenses. The rules were set by the Board of Internal Economy, a committee made up of representatives of all official parties in the Legislature. Acceptable expenses included such items as speech writing, postage, greeting cards, announcements using various forms of media, and items to give away such as mugs and pens with an MLA's name on them. Unacceptable expenses included material of a blatantly partisan nature, and material that solicited donations to a political party or attendance at political functions. The reason such items were not allowed was that they promoted the party itself, rather than facilitating its efficacy while representing the public in the Legislature. The disallowed items were expenses that should properly be paid out of party funds rather than money from the public purse. The rules for the Communication Allowance account allowed MLAs to request reimbursement for eligible items or services they had paid for out of their own pockets by attaching receipts to Request for Payment forms. Alternatively, bills could be paid directly by the Department of Finance if invoices were attached to the Request for Payment forms.

In the spring of 1987, after hearing a pitch from some of their leaders, most of the Tory MLAs bought into a plan to pool a portion of their individual Communication Allowances. The idea was to create a central fund to pay for advertising so the Tories could tell the people of their province what their government was doing for them and explain the government's position on highly controversial issues, such as privatization. The Conservatives wanted to do this using Grant Devine as their spokesperson.

The plan was enticing because some MLAs felt that the work done by the two companies that handled the bulk of the government's advertising—Dome Advertising and Roberts and Poole—was unsatisfactory and too expensive. As an example, they pointed to a brochure on health care that was produced in 1985. According to John Scraba, the MLAs were directed to contribute a portion of their Communication Allowances to pay for the brochure. Sources say the brochure was never circulated because nobody liked it. The MLAs were upset because they felt they had little say in how their contributed communication money was being spent. They thought that if a percentage of each MLA's allowance was pooled on a regular basis each year, the members would have more control over how their contributions were being allocated because the advertising campaigns would be discussed in caucus. Apparently a committee was formed to oversee the new pool, but it soon disbanded, and John Scraba was put in charge of implementing the plan.

The Tory plan called for each MLA to contribute up to 25 percent of his or her Communication Allowance each year. The money was to be used to pay for targeted advertising on television, on radio, or in newspapers. That first year most of the thirty-eight MLAs joined the pooling plan: some contributed more than 25 percent of their Communication Allowances, and some signed over most of their allowances. Over the next four years, all the Tory members participated in the pool at one time or another.

As long as the Communication Allowance was spent according to the rules laid down by the watchdog of the public purse at the Legislature, the Board of Internal Economy, pooling was an accepted practice. Under the rules, the communications work, such as radio advertising or newsletters, had to be completed before the bills were sent to Financial Services for payment. The problem was that some of the Tory invoices were being submitted before the work was done. Moreover, as the RCMP were to find out as their investigation progressed, only a portion of the pooled money was actually spent on advertising, the alleged purpose for collecting the 25 percent in the first place. As a result, the communications fund, which was supposed to contain only money that had already been spoken for, began to build up a surplus.

In late 1989, when the Tory invoices began to attract the attention of the people who processed the MLAs' Request for Payment forms at the Legislative Assembly Office, Gwenn Ronyk, the clerk of the Legislative Assembly, raised the issue of pooling with the speaker, Arnold Tusa. The Tory speaker replied that pooling Communication Allowances had gone on for years. He asked Ronyk if the NDP members were doing the same thing. Ronyk said they were. The NDP operated a communication pooling system through Phoenix Advertising, a Regina firm with close ties to the New Democrats. Ronyk pointed out, however, that the NDP invoices appeared to be for work that was actually done, but she wasn't sure that the same thing could be said about all the Tory invoices. In later court testimony, she explained:

The [invoices] from the opposition caucus were detailed in terms of what the product was that was being received, and it was from a company that was clearly in the communications business and was in the phone book advertising services. And the ones from the government caucus were very vague in terms of what was being purchased, what service was being provided, and they were from companies that I wasn't familiar with and nor were the Financial Services people.

Ronyk suggested to Tusa that the matter be discussed by the all-party Board of Internal Economy. Tusa, who also chaired the Board of Internal Economy, said the atmosphere in the Legislature at the time was so "poisoned" that it was hard to convene a meeting of the all-party committee to discuss the issue.

With Paul Raphael de Montigny's statement as a guide, the RCMP began to ask questions of their own about how the Tory caucus office was operating its pooling system. De Montigny had drawn the RCMP's attention to the companies whose names appeared on the invoices submitted with the Request for Payment forms.

"These communication accounts are computerized," Paul Raphael de Montigny told the police officer. "Marilyn did a check on the computer by doing a special sort by payee. She went back to 1982. (That was the year the Conservatives beat Allan Blakeney's New Democrats in a provincial election.) She found that the names of the companies that billed the members for communication services had changed over the years, but that the addresses for all of these companies remained the same. Marilyn checked through the phone book and other sources to try to ascertain that these were bona fide companies, but she couldn't."

One of the things that had aroused Marilyn Borowski's suspicions was the appearance of the invoices. Gwenn Ronyk was later to testify that the invoices "were the same size, the same border around it, a different colour perhaps, but they looked very similar. And they always came in a bundle, a bunch of them at the same time." De Montigny said that Borowski checked out the addresses of the companies that appeared on the invoices in the Henderson City Directory. It turned out that there was just one address for three or four different companies. "[Marilyn] found it to be for a firm of lawyers in Regina that she believes to be closely associated with the PC Party," de Montigny reported.

There were other things that had aroused Marilyn Borowski's suspicions. One of them was the form in which many of the requests for payment were submitted. Requests for payment submitted to the Finance Department were supposed to be accompanied by invoices or receipts for completed projects, in which case it would be reasonable to expect that the forms themselves would contain descriptions of the work done. Many of the Tory Request for Payment forms, however, were essentially blank, containing nothing more than the amounts requested and the MLAs' signatures. Any details about the transactions were on the accompanying invoices. The descriptions on the invoices were brief and were not broken down to show the nature of the work done. The wording also seemed to follow a predictable pattern, and there were no telephone numbers on the invoices.

Marilyn Borowski thought about this carefully after a chance meeting with a former Tory cabinet minister. De Montigny continued to lay it all out for the police officer: "Marilyn said that while attending a function she had a conversation with [a former Tory cabinet minister]. During this conversation, [he] mentioned that the PC Party has a special fund used to pay extra expenses." He told Borowski that requests for funds destined for this account were often processed using blank Request for Payment forms.

De Montigny reported that there was another minor incident that reinforced Marilyn Borowski's feeling that much more than just the pooling of Communication Allowances was going on. "At one time a ledger was maintained on the computer, listing the companies that received work from the government. This ledger made it very easy to see if there was patronage. Marilyn found that the routine printout of this ledger had been discontinued about the time the PCs took office, but that the program still existed in the computer system." De Montigny told the police officer that it was by printing this ledger that Borowski discovered that the different companies that appeared on the invoices all had the same address. Borowski told de Montigny she felt the fact that the PCs no longer had this ledger printed out, pointed to a cover-up.

Paul Raphael de Montigny said Marilyn Borowski told him and his wife that she believed blank Request for Payment forms signed by PC MLAs were being used to divert a portion of the MLAs' Communication Allowances into a PC Party central fund. She also told them she believed that most of the money was not being used for advertising at all but to build up a fund the party could use to fight the next election. De Montigny said Borowski told him: "Members will submit expense claims exceeding their actual expenses, but only up to their maximum allowable limit. These blank invoices allow this to be done. The money exceeding their actual expenses is then funnelled into this war chest." He said that Borowski mentioned that since 1982, about $400,000 to $500,000 had been paid out to members for communication expense claims. He said she didn't know what portion of the money had been diverted to the central fund.

De Montigny then told the police officer that Marilyn Borowski had also talked about a discussion she had with her boss, Gwenn Ronyk, the clerk of the Legislative Assembly. "Marilyn presented all of her facts to Ronyk. Ronyk's response was that it seemed like fraud was possible, but due to the [Legislative Assembly Office employees'] oath of confidentiality they could only report it to the Board of Internal Economy." He said Borowski told him and his wife that Ronyk believed that since the Board of Internal Economy comprised mostly PC government members, the whole thing would be covered up. He said Borowski did not mention when she had the conversation with Ronyk.

Paul Raphael de Montigny also told the RCMP officer that he was concerned that if the PCs found out he had talked with the police he might be fired from his job at SaskPower. "I don't know if I would lose my job, but I feel they [the PCs] would try. I feel that even my wife, or Marilyn, or even Gwenn would suffer. The attitude with the PCs is you are either with them or against them." When he was asked why he had chosen to come forward with this information at this particular time, de Montigny replied, "I have sat for eight years having heard and seen things like this, of a smaller degree occurring. This one was just too big to ignore."

"Do you know the names of any members that have submitted claims such as those contained in this statement?" the police officer asked.

"None specifically."

"Do you have any reason to believe individual members are

benefiting from this scheme?"

"I have no idea. I doubt it."

"Did Marilyn mention if she had a hard copy printout of the list of companies?"

"I think she did. I know she could get one generated again. This account is a part of public records."

Paul Raphael de Montigny then signed a copy of the statement he had given to the police.

The Police Investigation

With Paul Raphael de Montigny's statement in hand, officers at the RCMP subdivision headquarters in Regina checked the list of words available to them for new projects. These officers are in F division, so all their projects begin with the letter F. The name they finally decided to use was "Project Fiddle."

On July 30, 1991, just over three weeks after the police officer had talked with Paul Raphael de Montigny, two police officers interviewed two women at the Legislature in Regina: Gwenn Ronyk, the clerk of the Legislative Assembly, and Marilyn Borowski, the director of Financial Services. The police officers were interested in the Communication Allowances available to the members of the Legislative Assembly.

Marilyn Borowski told police that she had done some investigating and found that since 1987, three companies—Airwaves Advertising, Images Consulting, and Communications Group Advertising—had received hundreds of thousands of dollars from the Government of Saskatchewan. She said the companies were paid after they billed for communications services and that the payments were the result of requests submitted by members of the PC caucus. Borowski told the officers that the address used by all three companies was the address of a Regina law firm and that the three companies were not listed in the Regina telephone directory. She said after checking the payments made to the three companies, she discovered that approximately 25 percent of each PC caucus member's Communication Allowance entitlement had been given to at least one of the companies. Borowski told police that members of the opposition (the New Democratic Party) had not used these companies. The RCMP urged her to continue making inquiries, and suggested that she contact the law office whose address the companies were using to see if she could get answers to some of the things she considered strange.

On September 12, 1991, Marilyn Borowski informed the police that she had contacted the law firm and had spoken to a person she believed to be the receptionist. Borowski said she picked one of the companies, Airwaves Advertising, and asked to speak to someone who had knowledge of that company. She said she asked the person on the other end of the telephone about the company and was told that cheques for Airwaves Advertising went to the PC caucus. Borowski said she discussed her telephone conversation with Gwenn Ronyk, and the women decided she should call back and see if she could speak to someone who was responsible for one of the companies.

When she called back she was told that one of the lawyers would be able to answer her questions. She was told that he was busy at that moment but he would get back to her. When the lawyer called her back, she asked him about the companies and why the money was being sent to the law firm. Borowski said the lawyer told her he was not aware of any cheques coming to the law firm. According to Borowski, she then asked if there was someone else in the law firm who could answer her questions since he didn't appear to know what she was talking about. She said he promised to check around but doubted whether anyone would be able to help her because of lawyer/client confidentiality. Borowski said when the lawyer called her back, he told her that the client had instructed him to say that the cheques came to the law office because the numbered companies did work for MLAs all over the province and it was easier to send the cheques to one place.

Police officers searched the province's corporation branch records for all numbered companies in Saskatchewan with the same address as the law office and found four companies— 582806 Saskatchewan Limited, 582807 Saskatchewan Limited, 582808 Saskatchewan Limited, and 593297 Saskatchewan Limited. The first three companies were incorporated on April 23, 1987, and the last one was incorporated on February 26, 1990.

Corporation branch records showed that John Scraba,

communications director in the PC caucus office, incorporated 582806 and 582807 Saskatchewan Limited. The records also showed that Scraba and Joan Woulds, who was the administrator of the PC caucus office, were at various times directors and officers of the two companies. Police also learned that 582808 Saskatchewan Limited was incorporated by Woulds and Scraba, and that Woulds held the position of president, while she and Scraba were directors of the company at various times. Finally, Scraba also incorporated 593297 Saskatchewan Limited and he was the sole director for that company.

Through further investigation, the police learned that 582806 was known as Airwaves Advertising, 582807 was Images Consulting, 582808 was Communications Group Advertising, and 593297 was Systems Management Services. Systems Management was incorporated in 1990, the year before the Grant Devine Tories were defeated. It was John Scraba's private company even though it was set up in the same way as the other three.

Scraba says he set up Systems Management so he could sell computer software packages to Conservative candidates for the upcoming provincial election. He also planned to use the company to do other work for candidates and the PC Party. Scraba said that prior to the election, he was asked by Paul Staats, the director of communications for the premier's office executive council, if he had a company that could be used as a subcontractor for Dome Advertising, a company that received a large chunk of the government's advertising dollars. Scraba said he told Staats, who was responsible for dealing with all the government's advertising agencies, that he did. He then arranged to have lunch with Phil Kershaw, the president of Dome, to talk about what might be involved. Scraba said that to make sure that Staats and Kershaw knew he was serious about doing work for them using his own company, he billed Dome a consulting fee of $2,000 for the meetings. Scraba said Staats called Dome and asked that the bill be paid when it came in, and it was.

Before he was hired as communications director in the PC caucus office, John Scraba had worked in broadcasting. In the early 1970s, he was a disc jockey and sports announcer in a small town in Alberta. From there he moved to Saskatchewan, where he switched to news and sports. People in Moose Jaw and Saskatoon knew him by his on-air names, Jay Michaels or Jay King. Scraba made his Tory connections in Saskatoon through a man named Harry Baker, who would later become a Tory MLA. When Scraba first met him, Baker operated a small construction company and was head of the local small contractors' association. Scraba, who was the sports and news director at a private radio station, interviewed Baker for news stories. When Baker decided to enter politics in 1982, Scraba helped him with his campaign.

In the early 1980s Scraba took a run at the home construction business. There was a housing boom in Saskatoon at the time and he wanted to grab a piece of the action before it cooled down. He also became a partner in an Edmonton company that was involved in plastics. Neither of his business ventures paid off. The housing construction business in Saskatoon began to slip shortly after Scraba got into the market, and the plastic business in Edmonton didn't pan out. When the Tories were looking for a director of communications for their caucus office in 1985, John Scraba's name came up and Harry Baker put in a good word for him. The Conservatives hired Scraba in March 1985.

As director of communications, Scraba's job was to keep on top of political issues, especially controversial ones, and to advise MLAs on how to deal with them. He wrote news releases and helped with newsletters and brochures. He kept in touch with news outlets, making contacts that might help get stories aired, and helped prepare MLAs for interviews with the media. He set up a recording studio in his office at the legislative building and assisted MLAs in preparing radio news clips, which were sent to radio stations across the province. He also set up a video camera in his office and coached members on doing television interviews and giving speeches.

After the caucus meeting in Cypress Hills Provincial Park in the spring of 1987, John Scraba was directed to talk with a lawyer about setting up numbered companies to handle the money that would be collected in the communications pool. He was told to keep both the companies and the pool under wraps so the opposition and the media did not get wind of them. When the numbered companies were set up, Scraba ordered cheques, invoices, letterhead, and envelopes with the companies' names on them.

On October 7, 1991, three weeks before the provincial election, Gwenn Ronyk, the clerk at the Legislature, gave the police copies of Request for Payment forms with attached invoices submitted by the four companies between 1987 and 1991. She also gave them computer printouts of all payments made by the Government of Saskatchewan to the companies during that same period. The documents show that all thirty-eight Progressive Conservative MLAs had claimed communications services through one or more of the companies. The average claim was $22,062.

By January 10, 1992, the Conservatives had been out of office for nearly three months. Grant Devine was still their leader, but their ranks had been severely depleted and only ten MLAs had survived. Meanwhile, the police had received government cheques that had been deposited into bank accounts for the numbered companies set up in the caucus office. Altogether, the cheques added up to over $880,000.

The Tory caucus had been alerted to the police investigation in August 1991 when the RCMP had paid their surprise visit to John Scraba. While the RCMP commercial crime division was conducting its investigation, the Conservative caucus hired three lawyers to try to determine what had gone on in the caucus office. One lawyer represented the caucus, one represented Joan Woulds, and one represented John Scraba. On May 14, 1992, the lawyer representing the Tory caucus gave the RCMP a binder containing the fruits of his inquiry. It was difficult to piece together just what had happened because the books, ledgers, and account information relating to the business of the Progressive Conservative caucus had been shredded when the fall election was called. People in the caucus office, along with the lawyers, had to reconstruct the accounts from bank records. In his report to the police, the lawyer said they concluded that confidentiality and secrecy played a predominant role in dictating the Progressive Conservative caucus's methods of operation, including the lack of record keeping. The report further indicated that the incorporation of the numbered companies had occurred for the same reasons.

According to the report, all Progressive Conservative MLAs had contributed approximately 25 percent of their annual Communication Allowances to a central fund for advertising administered by the Progressive Conservative caucus. The lawyer said that it was the Progressive Conservative MLAs' perception that they were contributing to a "central fund" but in actuality, the 25 percent was being provided to the numbered companies. The lawyer's report said that Scraba was responsible for administering matters relating to the Communication Allowance contributions, for preparing and distributing materials, and for ensuring that payments were made.

The RCMP managed to pull together the following information. At a caucus meeting in Regina in March 1987, expense allowance requisitions were handed out, and thirty-three out of the thirty-eight Tory MLAs agreed to turn over a quarter of their Communication Allowances. Some of the MLAs recalled the requisition forms they signed were blank except for their names, while others believed the amount of the claims had been typed in. The forms were collected and sent to the Legislative Assembly Office, accompanied by invoices from Communications Group Advertising, one of the numbered companies set up by John Scraba on April 23, 1987. The invoices were all made out for "radio advertising." The Legislative Assembly Office approved the claims and sent thirty-three cheques totalling $85,957 to the numbered company's mailing address at the law office. The RCMP said the claims were improper because the numbered company had not bought radio time or performed any other service prior to the claims being submitted. Therefore, under the rules of the Legislature, a fraud had been committed. Police claimed the $85,957 was seed money to get the numbered companies and the fraud scheme up and running.

In January 1988, thirty-three of the thirty-eight MLAs signed on again, and they generated another $94,967 for the pool. The same thing was done in January 1989, May 1990, and March 1991, with a few minor variations. A different numbered company issued the invoices some years and some invoices were for newsletters, photo distribution, or video presentations instead of radio advertisements. While a handful of the Tory MLAs opted out of the pooling system each year, all thirty-eight participated at some point over the course of five years.

The RCMP officers working on Project Fiddle were sure they were investigating a fraud of massive proportions, but because of the missing records, they were having trouble building a case. They received an unexpected break on June 9, 1992. An official with the Canadian Imperial Bank of Commerce called the RCMP with news that bank employees had discovered a pile of $1,000 bills in a safety deposit box. The bank was closing two of its branches in Regina and moving into a new building. The bank sent letters to customers who had rented safety deposit boxes that had to be moved.

In early 1992, the bank sent a series of letters to Fred Peters, who had rented a safety deposit box at the Cornwall Centre branch of the CIBC, one of the branches being closed. Peters had paid the safety deposit box rental fee on March 29, 1990, giving his address as room 201 at the legislative building. On March 29, 1990, when Peters used the address on the application form for the safety deposit box, room 201 was an office of the Progressive Conservative caucus.

The letters sent to Fred Peters at the legislative building were returned unopened. The bank employee who called the Saskatchewan Legislature after the letters were returned was told no one by the name of Fred Peters worked there. Unable to contact Peters, the bank had the safety deposit box drilled open on April 10, 1992. Bank employees found $150,000 in $1,000 bills. The money was divided into three bundles—one with thirty bills and two bundles with sixty bills each. Each bundle was wrapped with an elastic band and was in an unsealed white envelope.

According to bank records, Fred Peters had entered the safety deposit box at 11:10 AM and again at 3:40 PM on March 29, 1990; at 11:45 AM on August 29, 1990; at 11:15 AM on October 31, 1990; and at 1:40 PM on January 31, 1991. Bank records showed that when Fred Peters was at the branch on January 31, 1991, he paid the 1991 and 1992 rental for the box with cash, and the employee accepting the payment said the man known as Peters said he was leaving the country for a while.

RCMP Corporal John Leitch was one of the officers assigned to investigate the safety deposit boxes. At the time, there was nothing to lead police officers to believe that the money in the safety deposit boxes was connected to the Tory fraud investigation. But that soon changed, and Leitch became the chief RCMP investigator for Project Fiddle.

After they discovered the first safety deposit box, bank officials searched their records for other accounts or safety deposit boxes opened by Fred Peters. Bank records showed that on September 11, 1991, a person using the name Fred Peters and the address 201 Legislative Building had rented safety deposit box number 813 at the bank's main branch in Regina. The records showed that Peters had only ever entered the box on that date. He had paid the rent until the end of 1992 and told the employee who took the rent money that he would not be around for a long time. Peters gave two telephone numbers on his application for the safety deposit box. One of the numbers belonged to the PC caucus office at the Legislature. The other number was for a cellular telephone registered to the Government of Saskatchewan. The cellular telephone was paid for by Airwaves Advertising, one of the four companies John Scraba set up in the Conservative caucus office. Safety deposit box number 813 contained ninety $1,000 bills. The police found a telephone number written on the edge of one of the bills. It was the number for Barb McLaren, the wife of caucus chair Lorne McLaren, when she worked in the caucus office.

The RCMP soon discovered that Fred Peters was the stage name once used by Frederick Peter Petrowich, who on March 29, 1990, the day the safety deposit box was rented at the Cornwall Centre branch of the CIBC, was employed as a personal assistant to Conservative Finance Minister Lorne Hepworth. Petrowich left the position of personal assistant in September 1990, but continued working for the Government of Saskatchewan with the Agricultural Development Fund Corporation in Regina. John Scraba had known Peter Petrowich as Fred Peters when they had both worked in private radio.

When police officers compared samples of Petrowich's handwriting with the handwriting on the safety deposit box applications, they found there were no similarities whatsoever. Police officers talked with Petrowich on February 5, 1992, and showed him copies of the safety deposit box applications. He said he hadn't opened the safety deposit boxes and knew nothing about them. Just as that trail was drying up, the RCMP got another break and another hot lead to follow.

A CIBC employee told police that the bank had received correspondence and two $20 bills from a person identifying himself as Fred Peters of Verona, Ontario. The employee said the writer asked that the bank renew the lease on safety deposit box number 813. The police asked the employee to keep the letter and the two $20 bills and to send Fred Peters a receipt for the money. The police officers then examined the signatures on the safety deposit box cards for both boxes and figured the same person made them. They also compared the writing with handwriting samples from John Scraba. They matched. And fingerprints found on the letter and the safety deposit boxes also matched fingerprints police had obtained from John Scraba, who by this time was a prime suspect in Project Fiddle.

Police officers tried to question a singularly uncooperative John Scraba in Verona, Ontario. Scraba had moved there after he lost his job when the Tories were defeated in the 1991 provincial election. The police tried several times to get a statement from him, but he refused. Police concluded that the money found in the safety deposit boxes came from money Scraba obtained from the MLAs' Communication Allowances via the numbered companies he had incorporated.

The RCMP were also interested in talking to Joan Woulds, who was the administrator in the Tory caucus office when John Scraba was communications director. Two RCMP officers talked with Woulds in the presence of her lawyer in Edmonton, Alberta, on September 7, 1992. She had moved there after the fall 1991 provincial election in Saskatchewan. Woulds said she knew nothing about the two safety deposit boxes at the CIBC. She did, however, know a lot about other things that went on in the Tory caucus office. In a statement to police, she said that she agreed to become an officer with signing authority for the numbered companies because the MLAs who were involved felt that it would be a conflict of interest for them to be officers of the companies. Woulds said she followed directions given to her by John Scraba, and that John Scraba followed the directions of a committee made up of Tory MLAs.

Back in Regina, RCMP officers were searching through the dozens of boxes of financial documents they had received from the Finance Department at the legislative building, including records for the PC caucus account into which the MLAs' grant money was deposited. Joan Woulds kept the records for the caucus account, which included a cheque ledger. Woulds, along with the caucus chair, caucus whip, and deputy whip, had signing authority for the caucus account. Two signatures were required for each cheque.

As the investigation continued, a connection between the caucus grant money and the pool of money collected from the MLAs' Communication Allowances emerged. Joan Woulds said that some time after the October 1986 election, for reasons of convenience, the PC caucus decided to make certain payments from the caucus account in cash. Woulds said the first time she needed to get cash from the bank, John Scraba gave her a ride to the bank in his car. About a month later, Scraba told her that he needed cash for the operation of the numbered companies. She said Scraba asked her if he could write a cheque from a numbered company to the caucus account and then have her withdraw an additional amount of cash in the same amount as the company's cheque. The money for the numbered companies would be on top of any money that Woulds would take out of the account to cover normal caucus office expenses. She said Scraba assured her that the caucus had approved doing it that way. From then on, Scraba got cash on a regular basis using that method.

Here is how the scheme was taking shape. The MLAs who had agreed to contribute up to 25 percent of their Communication Allowances to a central advertising fund signed Request for Payment forms on their Communication Allowances. These forms were gathered up and invoices from the numbered companies were attached. These requests for payment were then sent to the Department of Finance at the Legislature. The department paid the invoices and mailed the cheques to the numbered companies at the address of the law office. The cheques were then sent by courier to John Scraba, who deposited them into the numbered companies' accounts at the Royal Bank in Regina. Scraba would then write a cheque on one of the company accounts to the PC caucus account, and Joan Woulds would give him a cheque made out to cash payable from the PC caucus account. Scraba would go to the bank and deposit the cheque from the company into the caucus account. At the same time, he would withdraw cash from the caucus account using the cheque payable to cash signed by Joan Woulds and one of the other people in the caucus office with signing authority. A money-laundering scheme, passing money through the caucus account to hide the source, was in operation.

John Scraba cashed cheques ranging from $300 to $51,000 using that method. The police figure that $517,335 flowed from the numbered companies through the caucus account and into cash as a result of the scheme. And they believe that the $240,000 that was discovered in the CIBC safety deposit boxes came from that bundle of cash. That left another $277,000 unaccounted for. Employees at the Royal Bank where John Scraba cashed the caucus cheques said the caucus communications director received numerous $1,000 bills. The RCMP, by tracing serial numbers on $1,000 bills and examining the personal bank accounts of several PC MLAs, concluded that a substantial portion of the $277,000 went to Tory MLAs.

One of the first invoices John Scraba paid using one of the numbered companies and money collected from the members' Communication Allowances was a bill for $16,700 from Mercury Graphics for printing *Viewpoint*, the PC Party newspaper. This was in clear violation of the rules outlined in the members' handbook at the time, which prohibited Communication Allowance money from being used for a blatantly partisan purpose.

With the money-laundering scheme operating smoothly, John Scraba soon discovered ways to make extra money. His recording studio in the PC caucus office was equipped with state-of-the-art equipment paid for with caucus grant money. Scraba used the studio to produce radio advertisements for Tory MLAs. He then prepared phony invoices from the numbered companies, attached them to Request for Payment forms signed by the MLAs, and sent the forms to the legislative Finance Office for payment. The ads were produced using caucus equipment and caucus labour, so the only costs Scraba incurred were the fees he paid to radio stations to air the ads.

The beauty of the arrangement was this. A portion of the MLAs' Communication Allowances was purportedly being set aside to create a central fund to pay for radio ads by the premier. Scraba, however, incurred virtually no costs other than airtime for the radio ads he produced. Thanks to the numbered companies that collected money from the MLAs' Communication Allowances for radio advertising and the in-house audio equipment paid for by the provincial government, not only were the ads made, but the money collected to pay for them could be used elsewhere. The police investigation revealed that the numbered companies legitimately spent $229,059 on radio advertising between 1987 and August 1991. That's only a small portion of the over $837,000 in Communication Allowance money collected during that same period of time through the numbered companies.

Another way Scraba made money was by producing newsletters and brochures in the caucus office using caucus equipment and stationery supplied by the Legislative Assembly and then submitting Request for Payment forms and false invoices for payment through the MLAs' Communication Allowances.

Some Tory MLAs also went through Scraba and the numbered companies to buy computers, computer software, computer hard drives, video cameras, lecterns, and fax machines, all items that were ineligible under the rules for Communication Allowances. Not only that, but at times, the numbered companies made money on these transactions by charging MLAs more for the items than they paid for them. To cover up the fact that the claims were being made for ineligible items, the false invoices that accompanied these claims were for legitimate expenses such as newsletters, photo distribution, or video presentations.

The RCMP were interested in what was happening to the money after it was deposited into the accounts for the numbered companies. On August 6, 1992, two police officers interviewed John Gerich, a former Conservative MLA and PC caucus whip from 1986 to 1989. While he was caucus whip, he was one of the people who had signing authority for the PC caucus account. Gerich told police that he would frequently sign blank cheques drawn on the caucus account, but he said he had no knowledge of large sums of money taken out of the caucus account in cash.

The same day, two police officers also interviewed Michael Hopfner, who had taken over from Gerich as PC caucus whip. Hopfner also had signing authority on the caucus account when John Scraba worked in the caucus office. Hopfner said he, like Gerich, had on many occasions signed blank cheques drawn on the PC caucus account. Hopfner said he first learned about the large cash withdrawals from the PC caucus account earlier that year from the lawyer hired by the caucus office to investigate the way the caucus finances were being handled. He said he was told about the withdrawals when he and fellow Tories Lorne McLaren, John Gerich, Bill Neudorf, and John Weir met in the lawyer's office. Hopfner said no one at that meeting knew why the money was being taken out in cash or how it was being used.

Lorne McLaren, the member for Yorkton, a rural riding near the Manitoba border, was appointed caucus chair in January 1987. He held the job until the provincial election in October 1991, which made him caucus chair for most of the time John Scraba was communications director. Joan Woulds told police that in order to keep her account ledger balanced, she added in and out columns to represent the cheques received from the numbered companies and the cash taken out by John Scraba. She said she photocopied the ledger on a regular basis and gave the copies to McLaren. Joan Woulds also confirmed that at the time of the October 1991 election, most of the records relating to the PC caucus account that she maintained were destroyed.

The RCMP interviewed Lorne McLaren on August 20 and 21, 1992. Besides talking with him about pooling money and numbered companies, they questioned him about eight personal loans he had received from the PC caucus account. The cheque for the first loan was signed by Joan Woulds and John Gerich, who was caucus whip at the time. The police obtained a document headed "Personal and Confidential," which explained the terms of the loan. It read: "This will serve as a confirmation that the government caucus office has loaned the sum of $40,000 to Lorne McLaren, government caucus chairman on the 9th day of June, to be paid back in full at his earliest convenience." McLaren and Woulds signed the document about five months after McLaren took over as caucus chair. A paper attached to the document showed accumulated loans from the caucus to McLaren for $114,200. The other seven loan cheques were signed by Woulds and McLaren. The paper showed repayments totalling $1,144.75, including one for $500 that was made after a police officer contacted McLaren to arrange for an interview.

According to bank records obtained by the police, McLaren issued a cheque to the caucus for $5,000 dated September 11, 1990. They believed it was a payment on the loan. He gave the caucus another cheque, this one for $375, on February 6, 1991. He also gave the caucus two cheques for $4,000 each in the fall of 1990, but they bounced. McLaren, who was Joan Woulds's boss in the caucus office, told police Woulds was the only one aware of the loans at the time they were taken and that she had authorized them. Woulds pointed out that as McLaren was her boss, she didn't have the authority to authorize loans for him. Her story was that McLaren told her the PC caucus was aware of the loans and had approved them. She told police the first loan of $40,000 was to have been repaid in 390 days.

When two police officers interviewed a still-less-than-forthcoming John Scraba on September 1, 1992, in Verona, they asked him what he had done with the $517,335 in cash he had taken from the caucus account. He told them he had given it to Lorne McLaren. In fact, he had deposited $240,000 of it, in $1,000 bills, in two safety deposit boxes in branches of the CIBC in Regina. McLaren told police he knew nothing about the safety deposit boxes.

On September 18, 1992, the RCMP searched McLaren's

home in Fort Qu'Appelle, a resort community north of Regina. They were looking for cheque ledgers, bank statements, deposit slips, withdrawal slips, cancelled cheques, receipts, notes, memoranda, correspondence, loan applications, credit card statements, credit card slips, safety deposit box information, or anything else that could be related to Project Fiddle. They also obtained search warrants for banks where McLaren and his wife, Barbara, did their banking.

During the investigation, the RCMP discovered that in 1987 Lorne McLaren had authorized the transfer of $125,000 of PC caucus money to the PC Party of Saskatchewan to pay for polling. Although there was no system in place to check how caucus grant money was spent, the expectation was that it would be used to run the caucus office. The police believed that diverting it to Conservative Party coffers contravened the spirit in which this public money had been handed out. By this time, the RCMP were also investigating a report that $450,000 had been taken from the PC caucus account in late 1985 and deposited in a bank account in Martensville by veteran MLA Ralph Katzman. John Scraba had mentioned it during an interview with the RCMP. Joan Woulds had also told police about it.

As the police investigation progressed, other questionable activities were uncovered, this time involving the MLAs' Constituency Office and Services Allowances. In the late 1980s, MLAs were given between $860 and $1,089 a month to pay for constituency office clerical services, rent, furnishings, and supplies. If an MLA didn't spend the entire amount one month, he or she could carry it forward for future purchases within the year. Any unused amounts at the end of the year could not be carried over into the next year.

The police discovered that the PC caucus account had loaned one of the numbered companies $40,000 to buy computers for fourteen or fifteen MLAs for their constituency offices. Computers were acceptable items under the Constituency and Office Services Allowance; however, it is unclear whether it was proper to loan money from the caucus account to MLAs to buy constituency office equipment. Not only that, but false expense claims were used. The invoices stated "computer rental equipment" when in fact the computers were being purchased. The MLAs who received the computers signed Request for Payment forms under their Constituency Office and Services Allowances for $101 a month for thirty-six months to pay for the computers. The numbered company that was used as the intermediary to handle the computer purchases made money on the deal as it billed each member about $1,050 more than it paid for each computer.

The police investigation also uncovered that several PC MLAs and caucus employees received envelopes containing cash or additional cheques at the end of each month from the caucus account in addition to their regular salaries. Some former MLAs and caucus office workers said the extra fees were to top up salaries for extra work, although no deductions were taken off these payments. Some called these payments "expense allowances" even though the recipients weren't required to submit receipts. These "fee for service" payments cost taxpayers at least $61,000 a year, on top of the regular complement of salaries, expenses, and per diems. Lorne McLaren, the caucus chair, received $1,561 a month—$18,732 a year—in addition to his regular MLA salary and expenses. McLaren said he received the money because he was the chair of the PC caucus. McLaren's wife, Barbara, who worked in the secretarial pool in the caucus office, also received an expense allowance. She received $300 a month to start and later that was increased to $400. She said the money was compensation for errands she ran using her own vehicle and for extra hours she worked.

The whip and deputy whip also got money on top of their salaries. The whip got $7,759 a year, while the deputy whip received $3,880. Former MLA Michael Hopfner said he received cash or a cheque for $750 each month while he was whip and about $300 a month when he was deputy whip. Hopfner said he never claimed the money as income on his tax returns because it was an expense allowance; however, he wasn't required to submit receipts or otherwise account for the money. He said the allowance he received was to cover any out-of-the-ordinary expenses, even though the MLAs received expense allowances to cover travel costs and received per diems when the Legislature was in session and for caucus meetings.

John Gerich said he received seven $100 bills and one $50 bill in an envelope from caucus administrator Joan Woulds most months during his three years as whip. Sometimes he received a cheque. He said he used the money to pay for hotel rooms and gas. John Britton, who served as deputy whip for the final two years the Tories were in power, said he received $350 a month in cash or by cheque. Lorne McLaren said he signed "fee for service cheques" to top up the salaries of at least four employees in the caucus office. The director of caucus research received an expense allowance—initially $200 a month and later $750 a month—to hold parties for ministerial assistants in the Legislature. John Scraba received a fee for service payment of $7,000 a year. Joan Woulds received $500 a month for serving as president or a director for the numbered companies set up in the caucus office.

And some employees in the caucus office were on the payroll for Crown corporations or government departments. This meant government departments and Crown corporations were paying the salaries for people who were actually working in the caucus office. At one time, at least six ministerial assistants who were hired by a government department were working in the caucus office instead.

The story of the Tory fraud investigation did not break in the media until February 1993, nineteen months after Paul Raphael de Montigny told the police about the conversation he had had with Marilyn Borowski in the lounge at the Regina Inn. A couple of reporters who were in line at the cafeteria in the legislative building were chatting with a government employee. In the course of the conversation, the employee hinted that the RCMP were investigating the Tories and suggested the reporters might want to check it out. One of the reporters called the person in charge of the RCMP's commercial crime division in Regina, who confirmed that they were investigating at least three members of the Legislature for possible misuse of expense accounts. There were also unconfirmed reports that the RCMP were investigating both the New Democrats and the Conservatives. The police officer said they "were doing an investigation into some portion of expenses in relation to MLAs past." He wouldn't give any details.

When reporters followed up with the politicians, Bob Mitchell, the NDP justice minister, said he had been briefed about the existence of the investigation that January, but that he had not been provided with any details. Premier Roy Romanow would not comment on the investigation, but he did tell reporters that he was worried about the damage the investigation might do to the Saskatchewan Legislature. "These allegations place a cloud over the entire Legislative Assembly," he said. He felt the RCMP should produce "a thorough, swift, and speedy report" to clear the air as quickly as possible. The Conservative house leader, Bill Neudorf, would not comment.

It wasn't until October 1993, nearly nine months later, when news reporters got access to RCMP search warrants, that some details of the investigation became public. The search warrants showed the fraud investigation related to a period from January 1, 1987, to December 31, 1991, during which time the Conservatives were in government for all but two months.

Caucus Captain
Sinks with the Ship

Lorne McLaren had what most people would describe as a pretty good life before he got involved in politics. He had a good job, a decent salary, a loving family, a comfortable home, and a few businesses. He stood out for his community work in his hometown. But by the time politics was through with him, he was broke, unemployed, and behind bars in a federal penitentiary.

Lorne Aubrey McLaren was born at Aston, Saskatchewan, on August 17, 1928. He grew up on the family farm during the depression. In 1951, he got a job as a partsman at Morris Rod Weeder Incorporated, a farm implement manufacturing company located in Yorkton (a town in east-central Saskatchewan, not far from the Manitoba border). Twenty-eight years later, in 1979, he was appointed president of the company with a salary of $80,000 a year.

In the late 1970s, the Progressive Conservative Party was on the rise in Saskatchewan and was scouting for people who could win seats. There was an election just around the corner and the ruling New Democratic Party was out of favour with the voters, especially in rural areas. Lorne McLaren answered the Tories' call and in April 1982, when Grant Devine led his Conservatives to a smashing victory over Allan Blakeney's New Democrats, McLaren became the MLA for Yorkton. Shortly after the election, he was appointed labour minister. He was also given the job of overseeing two Crown corporations: SaskPower and the Potash Corporation of Saskatchewan. Having arrived in politics and having been made a cabinet minister to boot, McLaren quit his job as president of Morris Rod Weeder.

McLaren did not last long at the cabinet table in the new Conservative regime. In 1985, three years after he was appointed labour minister and a year before Devine went to the polls looking for a second term in office, McLaren was dropped from the cabinet. According to some political observers, he did not have what it takes to be a minister. When the premier put together his power team to sell the Tories to the people of Saskatchewan for a second time, Lorne McLaren was not among them.

McLaren was re-elected and shortly after the election, he was given a new job—caucus chair. It meant less power than a cabinet position and not as much take-home pay, but he got to handle a lot of taxpayers' money in the form of caucus grants. McLaren stayed in the caucus office until the 1991 provincial election, when he retired from politics.

On July 4, 1994, just short of three years after the Project Fiddle file was opened, the RCMP issued a news release stating that sixty-five-year-old Lorne McLaren had been charged with two counts of fraud over $1,000, one count of conspiracy to commit fraud, one count of theft over $1,000, and two counts of breach of trust. It was alleged that he had submitted false expense claims to get about $33,000 in cash from his Communication Allowance, diverted $125,000 from the caucus account to the PC Party, stolen $114,200 from the PC caucus bank account, and conspired with John Scraba to defraud taxpayers of $837,000. According to RCMP documents, the alleged offences happened between January 1, 1987, and October 31, 1991, when McLaren was caucus chair and had signing authority for the caucus bank account.

McLaren's preliminary hearing began on November 7, 1994. Eric Neufeld, the veteran Crown prosecutor assigned to the case, lined up sixty-four witnesses, a who's who of the former Conservative government and PC Party officials. The list included Grant Devine, Eric Berntson, and nearly every other member of the cabinet and government caucus from 1987 to 1991, including six sitting Tory MLAs. McLaren hired Neil Halford, who practised law in his home community of Fort Qu'Appelle, to defend him. Up until then, Halford had handled mostly real estate transactions.

The Crown's first witness was RCMP officer John Leitch, a twenty-one-year veteran of the force. Leitch is a tall, vigorous man with short Mountie hair and a keen eye for detail and numbers. Leitch got involved in the investigation part-time in 1991. He became involved full-time as chief investigator in the summer of 1992 after police found the $240,000 in the safety deposit boxes, and he was promoted from corporal to sergeant while working the case. Sitting in the witness box flipping through stacks of paper taken from brown file boxes and pulling up files on his laptop computer, Leitch laid out the police investigation and the Crown's case. He told the court his version of how the fraud scheme was set up. He gave details about the numbered companies, about the bank accounts for these companies, and about the false expense claims.

Sergeant John Leitch then talked about the money Lorne McLaren was alleged to have stolen from the caucus bank account. Leitch produced copies of caucus cheques payable to McLaren. The first cheque was for $40,000. Then there were cheques for $20,000, $15,000, $5,800, $13,000, $13,000, $3,900, and $3,500. The cheques added up to $114,200. The first cheque, the one for $40,000, was signed by Joan Woulds, the caucus administrator who kept the books when McLaren was given the cheques, and by caucus whip John Gerich, who also had signing authority on the caucus account. Woulds and McLaren, who of course had signing authority because he was caucus chair, signed the rest of the cheques. Leitch produced the June 9 letter confirming the loan. The police had found no record or evidence to indicate that there was a repayment plan with dates or interest to be charged, although Woulds had mentioned earlier that her understanding was that the $40,000 was to be repaid within 390 days. McLaren claimed the $114,200 was a loan and that he intended to pay it all back. Bank records showed that only $5,375 was ever repaid.

During Lorne McLaren's preliminary hearing, Sergeant John Leitch described the former cabinet minister and caucus chair as a man up to his eyeballs in debt who had bill collectors breathing down his neck. In the paper trail mapped by the RCMP, McLaren was shifting money from ten different bank accounts to handle payments as they came due. He was paying his bills with money he got from the caucus account and through false expense claims on his Communication Allowance. His personal bank account records between 1987 and 1991 were a litany of loans, credit card bills, lines of credit in arrears, and numerous rejections of refinancing proposals. He had accounts and loans at seven banks, two trust companies, and a credit union, plus six credit cards. He regularly transferred money between the accounts and regularly had cheques returned because the funds were not there to cover them.

Lorne McLaren's money problems started before he became caucus chair. In 1983, the year after he was first elected to the Legislative Assembly, McLaren, as part of a separation agreement that ended his twenty-two-year marriage to his first wife, admitted in affidavits filed in court that he was having money trouble. His businesses in Yorkton—a music shop and an apartment block—were losing money. McLaren, who was a cabinet minister at the time, was pulling in a salary of $62,000 a year, plus $5,000 a year in expense money. He also had access to an unlimited travel budget. According to the affidavits, he was getting a net income of $3,383 a month. The terms of his 1984 divorce gave his ex-wife a $75,000 lump-sum settlement and a maintenance payment of $2,100 a month. McLaren's salary dropped when he lost his cabinet seat in 1985, but his pay cheque went up again when he became caucus chair the following year. On top of his MLA salary, he received approximately $1,560 per month as caucus chair. Crown prosecutor Eric Neufeld, who has a flair for the theatrical and a sharp, stabbing way of throwing unsuspected probing questions at nervous witnesses, told the court that the evidence of McLaren's credit cards showed that his penchant for the "good life" was the root of his downfall.

Not only did Lorne McLaren help himself to taxpayers' money, but he dished out a sizeable chunk—$125,000—to the PC Party of Saskatchewan to help pay for polling. When RCMP officers searched McLaren's home in Fort Qu'Appelle, they came across a confidential letter from PC Party President Ron Barber to McLaren dated January 30, 1987. Barber wrote, "This is to acknowledge receipt of a loan to the Progressive Conservative Party of Saskatchewan in the amount of $125,000. Terms of the agreement for repayment are as discussed. Thank you for your support at this time." The $125,000 was registered in the PC Party's ledger in February 1987 as a donation.

Lorne McLaren's preliminary hearing to see if there was enough evidence to go to trial was scheduled to last for three weeks, but it lasted only six days and many of those on the witness list were never called to testify. McLaren said he stopped the preliminary hearing because he couldn't afford to pay a lawyer to keep it going, especially as he would most likely have to pay more legal bills for a trial.

McLaren's trial began on May 15, 1995. This time Crown prosecutor Eric Neufeld had lined up more than one hundred witnesses. The list included thirty-seven present and former Tory MLAs, eleven of whom were also facing fraud-related charges as the result of Project Fiddle. Court of Queen's Bench Justice Isadore Grotsky, a veteran judge, was assigned to hear the case. The Crown had collected more than five hundred exhibits, which were stacked in a bookcase and boxes in the courtroom. The trial was expected to last at least six weeks. "I'm just darn glad I got a chance to defend myself right now," McLaren told reporters as they circled him on the courthouse steps when he arrived for the start of his trial.

Later that day, talking with reporters outside the courthouse, McLaren's lawyer, Neil Halford, said the first few hours of the trial were "really complicated." He reported that there were mountains of paper in the courtroom, along with computers and overhead projectors, and that it was getting hard to follow what was going on. He added that by the end of the trial, he expected to be "buried up to the shoulders" in paper.

Neil Halford described Lorne McLaren as a good man. "I think everyone who knows him would say he is an honest and decent person. I think he is going to have to take the stand and try to show that he didn't have a lot of control over what the other people were doing."

"I pleaded not guilty and that is the way I stand," Lorne McLaren told reporters during the lunch break on the first day of his trial. "They are going to sure have to prove it."

Just over a week into the trial, Lorne McLaren dismissed Neil Halford. The reason given the court was that the demands of a long trial were too much for Halford, who worked alone in his law office at Fort Qu'Appelle. McLaren considered acting as his own lawyer, but Justice Grotsky strongly recommended against that. McLaren had earlier applied for legal aid but had been turned down because his income exceeded the limit for legal aid. The limit was $900 income per month; McLaren received $1,239 a month from his MLA pension.

It took a few days, but McLaren found a new lawyer, David Birchard, who practised law in Regina. The case was adjourned for three weeks to give Birchard time to get up to speed. When the trial resumed, it lasted for only a few days. Once again, most of the witnesses did not have to testify. On June 27, 1995, Lorne McLaren pleaded guilty to three of the six counts in the indictment against him: the fraud charge involving over $837,000 of public money, the charge of diverting $125,000 to the PC Party, and the charge of stealing $114,200. The other three charges were stayed, which meant that if they weren't brought back within a year, they would be dropped. McLaren was given a few months to get his affairs in order before the sentencing hearing.

"She's been a process," he told reporters as he left the courthouse. His wife, Barbara, stood by his side. "It's getting to the point where I wish the heck it was all over. Anyway, come and hear us at the [sentencing] hearing and then I'll tell my story. I haven't had a chance to tell my story yet." He laughed but it was a nervous laugh. If the trial had continued, McLaren would have had the option of testifying when the defence presented its case. With the guilty plea, McLaren did not have the opportunity to address the court; however, he could choose to make a statement before the judge at his sentencing hearing.

"You'll tell your story [at] the hearing?" a reporter asked.

"We can call witnesses then. I'll be on the stand then," McLaren replied.

When it was his turn to face reporters, Crown prosecutor Eric Neufeld said Lorne McLaren was not given a deal in return for his guilty plea. "We were ready to proceed and slug it out,"

Neufeld said. "But it's nice to have that part of the case out of the way. It's a long hot summer," he added. "And it would be a long time to have to go through all of this evidence. But it's a sad day for Mr. McLaren."

During the sentencing arguments that started on November 11, 1995, Saskatchewan taxpayers got their first chance to learn details about some of the activities uncovered by Project Fiddle. In his arguments before Justice Grotsky, Eric Neufeld talked about the deals Lorne McLaren had made with John Scraba. There was a 1988 Pontiac Tempest purchased in June 1988 by one of the caucus companies for just over $16,000 and used by John Scraba as his personal car. One of the caucus companies also paid for the licence and insurance. In August 1991, McLaren had signed a bill of sale giving the car to Scraba for $100.

Then there was evidence of another alleged agreement between Lorne McLaren and John Scraba, this one for a lot more money. Scraba said it was a legitimate deal, even if McLaren did not see it that way. The so-called agreement was explained in a letter Eric Neufeld produced for the court. It was dated June 15, 1988, and signed by McLaren. It said:

This agreement acknowledges and provides authority for John Scraba to receive remuneration for various communications services rendered to the PC caucus members. Such services shall be for duties carried out pertaining to 582808 Saskatchewan Limited; 582807 Saskatchewan Limited, 582806 Saskatchewan Limited which were set up on behalf of PC caucus. A 10 percent communication fee may be charged for Mr. Scraba's services. Such amount to be paid at any time mutually agreed upon by Mr. Scraba and the caucus chair, or prior to the next provincial general election.

Ten percent of the money handled by the three numbered companies from the time they were set up by John Scraba in April 1987 until the time they were closed down in the fall of 1991 came to approximately $90,000, the amount the RCMP found in safety deposit box number 813 at a Regina branch of the Canadian Imperial Bank of Commerce. This was the box that

Scraba had rented under the assumed name of Fred Peters on September 11, 1991, approximately one month before the provincial election that saw the Tories voted out of office.

Lorne McLaren had a few different stories on this one. One time he said he never saw the letter before the RCMP showed it to him, and that John Scraba must have forged his signature. Another time, he said he signed the letter but thought someone else had approved the deal. And on another occasion he said Scraba most likely slipped the letter in with other documents he had given him to sign, and he signed it without realizing what it was.

At the sentencing hearing, Eric Neufeld argued that Lorne McLaren not only knew about the fraud scheme being run out of the Tory caucus office, but that he helped set it up and had his hand in most of what went on. Neufeld described McLaren as a person who was instrumental in making the rules and therefore knew he was breaking them. "He was elected to serve the public and not to cheat them or to steal from them," Neufeld added. "The accused abused the trust placed in him for both personal and political ends. [Elected officials] are trustees of the public purse. They are accountable, and they will be called to account." He went on to say, "He's brought shame on our house. His conduct could not help but hurt the public's confidence in our elected officials and our democratic institutions."

Crown prosecutor Eric Neufeld asked Justice Grotsky to send Lorne McLaren to jail for three to five years. He also asked him to order McLaren to pay back the remainder of the $114,200 he stole from the caucus account and the $125,000 he diverted from the caucus account to the PC Party of Saskatchewan. Neufeld then turned to the over $837,000 that police said was obtained from MLAs' Communication Allowances by means of a fraudulent scheme involving the numbered companies in the caucus office. Neufeld was willing to give McLaren credit for the $240,000 that the RCMP had recovered from the two safety deposit boxes, but he argued that because McLaren was one of the key people behind the scheme, he should be responsible for paying back the rest—over $600,000. He said the former caucus chair could sue other

Tories who were involved in the fraud scheme with him, to help pay the debt.

Lorne McLaren's lawyer, David Birchard, came to the sentencing hearing armed with a doctor's report, a bundle of letters of reference, and an apology. "Nobody in this courtroom feels worse than Mr. McLaren, except his family," Birchard said. "He has instructed me to give to the court his abject apologies. Mr. McLaren knows and admits he was derelict in his overall duties to supervise caucus and taxpayers' money in order to ensure it was spent properly. Mr. McLaren does not deny he was the captain of the caucus ship, and he must bear the responsibility for the excesses that occurred and that he directly benefited from the scheme. His fall from grace is complete. He is financially destitute. His savings are gone, and he faces a mountain of debt."

According to Birchard, McLaren had a monthly income of $2,783, which included his MLA pension of $1,239. He had assets of $9,400 and debts of $96,000. Birchard said McLaren was suffering from hypertension and diabetes, and in February 1994, he suffered a stroke and was being treated for high blood pressure. Birchard asked the judge for a sentence of less than two years and that McLaren not have to pay restitution.

Justice Grotsky said he had given the question of restitution serious thought and, according to his figures, if McLaren applied every penny of his total monthly income on the outstanding balance, it would take in excess of two hundred years to pay it off. "I have here a man who is sixty-seven, who is not in good health according to the medical reports and whose ability to make repayment is virtually nil," Justice Grotsky said. He also noted that the Supreme Court of Canada says where there is no chance of recovering money, there is no sense in making an order for repayment. He then asked McLaren if he had anything to say before he was sentenced.

Standing in the prisoner's box, looking straight at the judge, his shoulders slumped, Lorne McLaren said, "All I can say, Your Honour, is [that] I agree with what Mr. Birchard has said, that I did communicate that with him, [and] that I am very, very sorry with the affairs that have taken place over the last five years.

I apologize for them. Whatever sentence you subject me to, I fully intend to serve that without any appeal." Justice Grotsky put off sentencing until two o'clock the next day.

Lorne McLaren faced a troop of reporters and television cameras when he left the courthouse. "I'm not going to talk about it at all today, thank you very much," McLaren told the journalists, his voice cracking. He kept walking as the reporters closed in around him, shouting over each other while throwing a barrage of questions at him.

"You have a chance to express your sorrow and remorse now, Mr. McLaren," one reporter shouted.

"I did it in court today."

"Do you regret your decision to get into politics?" another reporter asked.

"Nope."

The lenses of television cameras followed McLaren as he got into a car and was driven away.

McLaren was a little more talkative when he returned to court for sentencing the next afternoon. His wife, Barbara, and several members of her family were with him.

"We're just waiting to see what it's going to be," he told the reporters who were waiting for him in front of the courthouse. "We're prepared to take whatever comes."

"What did you do last night, Mr. McLaren?"

"Slept."

"How did you sleep?"

"Good."

"So, how do you feel about it all today?"

"Great. Yeah, great. It's coming to an end."

"How difficult is it going to be for you and your family?" a reporter asked.

Before he could respond, his wife, Barbara, turned and faced the reporter, anger in her eyes. "What do you think, for God's sake? How stupid," she said tersely. She took her husband's arm and led him up the courthouse steps.

Inside, the courtroom was nearly full. About half of those in the room were reporters. Lorne McLaren sat in the prisoner's box to the right of the judge. An RCMP officer sat on a chair against the wall just to McLaren's left. Justice Grotsky summarized the case as he saw it, and talked about the factors he had considered in determining the sentence: deterrence, McLaren's financial situation, his health, and his age. Justice Grotsky then asked McLaren to stand. "It is difficult to understand how a person with your background could have become involved in this type of criminal activity," Justice Grotsky said, looking straight at McLaren. "You, by your criminal misconduct, have brought our cherished legislative process into disrepute." He accused McLaren of creating "cash cows" to illegally and fraudulently plunder the provincial treasury and through it the people of Saskatchewan. "If those who make the law do not observe it, who will?" he asked.

On the big fraud charge of over $837,000, Justice Grotsky sentenced McLaren to three and a half years in prison. On each of the two other charges, diverting $125,000 to the PC Party and stealing $114,200, McLaren was sentenced to two and a half years. The sentences were to be served concurrently. Dealing with the question of restitution, Justice Grotsky said, "There is no realistic prospect of payments." He said it was up to the Crown to sue if it wanted to try to recover the money.

When the judge left the courtroom, the RCMP officer who was sitting next to McLaren took him by the arm and handcuffed him. McLaren's wife, Barbara, surrounded by family members and friends, struggled to keep back the tears. McLaren talked with his lawyer for a few minutes before he was led away.

Downstairs in the courthouse, McLaren was told to empty his pockets. An RCMP officer took the money McLaren had with him, the rings he had on his fingers, including his wedding ring, and his watch. While McLaren was being processed for prison, reporters interviewed Eric Neufeld on the sidewalk outside the courthouse.

"Are you satisfied with that sentence?"

"It's certainly within the range that I was specifying. I guess whether I'm satisfied or not really makes very little difference. I was very pleased. I thought it was a very well-reasoned, articulate judgement. And [it] really hit all the issues that had to be addressed."

When asked what the sentence meant for the other Tory fraud cases that were to come before the courts, Neufeld said that although it set a precedent, every case was different. Reporters, photographers, and television camera operators then headed for the back entrance to the courthouse, where Lorne McLaren would be brought out and placed into a waiting RCMP van.

"Do you have any regrets, sir?" a reporter asked, when a handcuffed McLaren came through the door and was directed toward the van by two RCMP officers.

"Yes, I do," he replied.

McLaren was hurried into the police van and driven to the Regina Correctional Centre, just east of the city. There he was told to take a shower, given yellow prison clothes, and then locked up in a cell by himself. He spent a week at the correctional centre before being transported to the federal penitentiary in Prince Albert, about a five-hour drive north of Regina. Prince Albert is the prison where hardened criminals like serial killer Clifford Olson are kept in a tight security section known as the "shoe."

Shortly after he arrived at the P.A. pen, as it's known locally, Lorne McLaren was transferred to Riverbend, a minimum-security facility a stone's throw from the high wire fence surrounding the penitentiary. A few weeks later, McLaren agreed to an interview in the medical centre of the Riverbend facility to discuss his side of the story.

"It's coolish out there," McLaren said as he walked into the medical examination room. The guard who had brought him left and let the door slam behind him. Just beyond the window, a group of men standing outside the building puffed on cigarettes. It had snowed overnight and a blanket of wet snow covered the ground. McLaren sat on a chair facing a microphone and a tape recorder set up on a wooden table. He seemed nervous.

"I've had a lot of mail from friends and relatives over the last few weeks, so I've been trying to respond to all of them. To let them know I'm still kicking and living." He forced a laugh. At first, he was reluctant to talk. He said he just wanted to do his time, get out, and not cause any trouble. After assurances that the intent was not to get him in any trouble, he relaxed a bit and agreed to record the interview.

McLaren talked about the RCMP investigation, his preliminary hearing, and his trial. "I was so fed up with four years [of the investigation]. And getting broker and broker by the day. My preliminary was supposed to last six weeks. And after the sixth day of sitting there and listening to that—90 percent of it was everybody else's name, nothing to do with me . . . —I thought, heck, I might as well go straight to trial. It cost me $50,000 in lawyer's fees." After some prodding, he continued, "I pleaded guilty and got on with my life. So that's what I did."

He recalled his first days behind bars at the Regina Correctional Centre. "You're locked up twenty-three and a half hours a day. Your meals are shoved under your door. [You're] let out a half-hour to exercise, go walk around in the courtyard outside, every day. Not every day. Yeah, I guess you could go if you wanted to. Then a couple of the days, you were let out for a half an hour but in that time you had to shower and make any phone calls that you wanted to make." He spoke slowly and softly as he rubbed his hands together.

McLaren then talked about his transfer to the Prince Albert penitentiary and on to Riverbend. "There were no beds in A-1, A-2, which is—they call it the fish tank—for everybody who comes in, the first go-a-round. [Then] you get assessed and you get moved to maximum security or medium security, minimum security, or whatever. So, because there were no beds, I was thrown into segregation. And that was twenty-three hours a day in the cell and an hour to walk around outside."

Of Riverbend, he said, "It's great here. This job that I work at, morning and afternoon, passes the day. I get five dollars a day." He laughed. "I help with the cleaning of the officer's mess at the front of the penitentiary. And another guy works with me, the two of us. It's a fairly big building that we go through, make sure the tables are all ready for their meals. Mopping the floor, cleaning, garbage out, so on. I'm doing what I'm told to do," he said. "Just do my time and get out."

He admitted that at times just doing time was not as easy as it sounded. "Like, I cried one day. You're allowed one phone call a week inside the pen there. And there's five or six hundred people and there's six phones. So, you put your request in. And most of the time you can get through. But when you phone, how do you know your wife is sitting at home? She's not there all the time waiting for your gall darn phone call, because you don't know exactly what day you may be calling and you can't tell her that [you're] going to call her on such and such a day. And just to try and set up a visit, it takes a month to get somebody cleared."

He recalled the trouble his wife, Barbara, and her daughter had setting up a visit. It was Barbara's first visit to the Prince Albert penitentiary. They hadn't seen each other in five weeks. Eventually, Barbara and her daughter were allowed inside the penitentiary, but McLaren had to visit with them with a glass wall between them. He explained: "You phoned back and forth. I bawled when I got out of there that day, to myself. You see it in movies, but when you get in there and do it, can't kiss them, can't hug them, can't do nothing. You just sit there and talk. Tears came." The visits after that were a lot better. McLaren and his wife even got to spend most of a weekend together. During some visits, they spent hours playing cards.

Lorne McLaren also talked a bit about what happened in the Tory caucus office while he was caucus chair. The whole idea of pooling money, he said, was to get the premier on radio and television more often to get the same message out, right across the province. There was lots of money to do it with. "The grant money kept coming every month, whether you needed it or not," McLaren said, referring to the caucus grants. Many Conservatives felt those grants came with no strings attached and could be spent on advertising, even partisan advertising, with no questions asked. "What would it have been like in the first term? I haven't a clue because I wasn't in the caucus office then when we had fifty-five MLAs. We had thirty-eight when I was there, and you couldn't spend that much money."

The former labour minister admitted he ran a loose ship when he was caucus chair. He said he was too busy doing his MLA work to keep tabs on the day-to-day running of the caucus office. He said he relied on the office administrator, Joan Woulds, and the communications director, John Scraba, to do that. He admitted he had to carry some of the blame for what happened, especially the $114,200 he took from the caucus bank account in a so-called loan. "I took that money, personally," he said. "Even though I signed a promissory note and I've been paying money back, it didn't matter. Even if I'd paid it all back by now, it was still wrong because I took it in the first place. But this other stuff," he let out a big sigh, "defrauding the public of [nearly] a million and that $125,000." McLaren said he had been reluctant to give the $125,000 to the PC Party of Saskatchewan. He said he did it because the request came from higher up. "I didn't know if I had the right to say no," he explained. "I was getting a letter saying they [the PC Party] got it and would pay it back, that it's a loan. That's the last I thought of it. . . . When your bosses ask for something, you don't tell them to fly a kite. At least I never did."

Shortly after Lorne McLaren pleaded guilty, the provincial Conservative Party paid back the $125,000 to the province's Finance Department, but the PCs said that didn't mean the party admitted to any legal wrongdoing. The money for the repayment came from the PC Metro Fund, a pool of money administered by a handful of Tories at arm's length from the party. The list of contributors is kept secret. The Metro Fund is believed to have contained at least a couple of million dollars at the time the $125,000 was paid to the Finance Department.

McLaren also talked about John Scraba's car. At the trial, Scraba said when he asked McLaren if he could get a car, he had just declared bankruptcy after his house construction company in Saskatoon had gone under and it was hard for him to get credit. Scraba said McLaren indicated to him that he didn't want other MLAs in the caucus office to know he was getting this perk. McLaren acknowledged signing the letter giving Scraba the Pontiac Tempest for $100, but he said he couldn't recall whether he gave approval for Scraba to buy the car in the first place. He said, laughing, "I guess what I thought was, caucus had bought that car for him." McLaren said he thought the car could be part of Scraba's severance package. All the polls at the time showed the Tories were in deep trouble and very few of the

MLAs would survive the election. McLaren said he assumed that Scraba would be out of a job. "So, I said, give me a hundred bucks and you can keep the car."

Before McLaren's trial, Scraba had told police that after he learned of their investigation, he asked McLaren what he should do with the money he was "holding in safekeeping." Scraba said McLaren told him not to go near it. In the prison interview, McLaren said he didn't know the money existed until it came out in court, and that he never had this conversation with Scraba.

Lorne McLaren was given day parole in May 1996, after spending about eight months behind bars. He was granted full parole six months later. Even though he was out of prison, he was still not off the hook. The police investigation was continuing and Crown prosecutors were getting ready to put more Tories on trial. Lorne McLaren would have to testify at some of those trials.

The Saddle
and the Kickback

There were two other trials involving politicians that were making the news just as Project Fiddle was getting up steam. They were not part of Project Fiddle, but they indicate the climate of the times. One involved Progressive Conservative MLA Gerald Muirhead and the other involved New Democratic MLA Murray Koskie. Both had to do with the MLAs' use of taxpayers' money. Even though both cases concerned MLA Communication Allowances, the transactions had nothing to do with John Scraba, his numbered caucus companies, or the PC caucus office. Muirhead and Koskie committed their frauds on their own.

Former Tory MLA Gerald Muirhead (better known as Gerry to his friends and even to a lot of people who have just heard of him) is a self-described cowboy. In early January 1995, at the age of sixty-three, he was convicted of fraud. Muirhead's downfall came because of a complaint from a Liberal in his constituency of Arm River, an hour north of Regina. The complaint centred around a custom-made saddle, saddlebags, a breast collar, and a sash with Muirhead's name on it. He had bought the gear for his horse with taxpayers' money.

Gerald Muirhead, a tall, muscular man who always seemed to know all the gossip circulating at the Legislature, was first elected in a by-election in 1978. He was re-elected in 1982, 1986, and 1991. When the Tories were in power in the 1980s, Muirhead served as the minister responsible for Saskatchewan crop insurance and as legislative secretary to Premier Grant Devine, who was also the agriculture minister at the time. Later

Muirhead was given the job of legislative secretary to the minister of justice. He was an MLA for eighteen years—one of the longest-serving members in the Saskatchewan Legislative Assembly. He liked to brag about his longevity as a politician. He was also quite taken with his saddle.

"I used it in parades for '89, '90 and '91," Muirhead said, leaning against the saddle, which hung in a shed on his farm near Craik. The interview took place in December 1993. A few days earlier, the RCMP had charged Muirhead with fraud and breach of trust as he left police headquarters in Regina after being interviewed about Project Fiddle. He was facing one count of fraud over $1,000 and one count of breach of trust.

The RCMP accused Muirhead of using a false expense claim to get the money for the saddle and the accessories that went with it. He had purchased the outfit in 1988 for $2,265. The Request for Payment form and the invoice sent to the Legislative Assembly for payment listed the saddle and accessories as "parade equipment." On the invoice, the saddle was described as a sign made for a vehicle to be used in parades. According to the police, the false invoice for the equipment was paid for with money from Muirhead's Communication Allowance. Under the rules of the Legislature, saddles were not acceptable expenses under the Communication Allowance.

"I'd put on quite a show at parades," Muirhead said, rubbing the saddle with his right hand. "I'd fill these bags here full of candy—usually two- or three-hundred-dollars' worth to give out to kids at the fairs."

During the interview, he said he had pictures of himself on his horse in a parade in Craik. He agreed to go into the house to get one. He soon returned with a large framed picture of himself on horseback wearing the sash with his name on it and carrying the bags of candy. Muirhead said he felt the money he had put into the parade gear had been well spent. "I want that horse to put on a good show," he said, pointing to the picture. The television camera panned and zoomed from Muirhead to the picture and back again. "That horse is so well trained. I get it cantering on a light lope. Go across the street and up on people's lawns and I throw it [candy] out to older people. It has been said that between twelve thousand and fifteen thousand people have viewed me in parades. And I've bought mugs for $2,000 that one thousand people get. I thought this was a good deal." During his trial in early 1995, Muirhead told Court of Queen's Bench Justice Ron MacLean that he thought his spending $2,265 on the saddle and accessories was no different from other politicians spending money on promotional mugs or scarves.

Crown prosecutor Eric Neufeld argued that Muirhead knew that if he submitted an expense claim for a saddle, the financial clerks at the Legislative Assembly would turn him down. "I would submit he needed a way to disguise it and came up with the phrase 'parade equipment' and used that concept in a deceptive manner to get the saddle and its accessories paid for with public funds," Neufeld told the judge.

Muirhead's lawyer, Mike Megaw, characterized the trial as a "credibility contest." Megaw argued that it was absurd to suggest Muirhead tried to hide the fact his claim for parade equipment included a saddle. Muirhead admitted he knew a saddle was not an acceptable Communication Allowance expenditure, but thought his claim should be treated differently because it was part of parade equipment intended for advertising. The owner of the store where Muirhead purchased the saddle told police that Muirhead asked him not to write "saddle" on the invoice and instead said he should describe the purchase as "parade equipment." He also didn't want him to tell anyone about the sale.

After hearing all the witnesses and all the arguments, Justice MacLean found that Muirhead had failed to properly disclose his saddle purchase, and he was therefore guilty of fraud. In handing down sentence on January 23, Justice MacLean said that Muirhead was evasive when he was on the stand at the trial, and he did not believe everything Muirhead told the court. He summarized, "In my view, it was just plain nonsense and was a feeble attempt to justify his actions." He fined Muirhead $5,000. The breach of trust charge was stayed. Muirhead was allowed to keep the saddle and its accessories.

Outside the courthouse, Muirhead protested his innocence: "I stand before God and man and said everything absolutely true, and I say I am absolutely innocent, and I can't say anything more than that. I'm absolutely innocent." The next day, Gerald Muirhead was kicked out of the Saskatchewan Tory Party. The Conservative leader at the time, Bill Boyd, said the party had no choice because Muirhead refused to step down voluntarily. Muirhead kept his MLA salary and decided to sit in the house as an independent MLA while he appealed his conviction to a higher court. He did not run in the 1995 provincial election.

Muirhead took his case to the Saskatchewan Court of Appeal, but his plea of innocence didn't stand up there either. "I'm really disappointed," he told reporters outside the courthouse. "We've been working sixteen months on this appeal. I guess I'm the only individual, myself and God knows that I'm telling the truth and that's why I'm pushing this thing. It's one person's word against another." He tried an appeal to the Supreme Court of Canada but was rejected there as well.

Gerald Muirhead blamed his saddle troubles on his political opponents, mostly Liberals. He said they went to the RCMP three weeks and two days before the 1991 election and made up stories about him and his family. He said they did it in an attempt to discredit him in his constituency of Arm River to try to win votes. His allegations were never proven, but it was generally accepted in Craik, the town near his farm, that Gerald Muirhead had lots of enemies (Liberals and New Democrats among them) and every once in a while threats of lawsuits would fly around coffee row in the small farming community. Although he was nabbed with the saddle, Muirhead was not caught up in the Project Fiddle net. He contributed some of his Communication Allowance to the communication pool, but he didn't run any false expense claims through John Scraba or his numbered companies.

Murray Koskie was the other MLA nabbed for fraud that was unrelated to the Tory fraud scandal. It just happened that he was pulled in while the RCMP were conducting their investigations. Koskie was a New Democrat, and he was charged with taking a kickback.

In June 1993, a reporter received a tip that the RCMP were investigating some sort of wrongdoing by Koskie. Koskie couldn't be found to comment. Early the next morning, Premier Roy Romanow issued a press release announcing he had accepted Koskie's resignation as minister of highways and transportation. Koskie would keep his seat in the Legislature while the allegations worked their way through the justice system. In a letter to the premier, Koskie wrote that the police investigation involved expenditures during his time in opposition. That, of course, was when the Conservatives were in power and the PC caucus office scam was up and running. The RCMP commercial crime section issued a release confirming officers were "investigating circumstances relating to the Communication Allowance of Murray Koskie." No details were given.

Koskie, at age sixty-four, had served in both Allan Blakeney's and Roy Romanow's cabinets, and he was one of the longest-serving MLAs in the Legislature. He was first elected in the rural constituency of Quill Lakes in 1975. When the NDP was in power in the 1970s and early 1980s, Koskie served as the minister of social services and minister of consumer affairs.

The sworn statement used by police to get a search warrant in May 1993 alleged that in March 1991, a company Koskie had hired for communications consulting billed the provincial government for $1,250 with the intention of paying the money back to Koskie. The statement also said that an invoice sent to the province for payment had been backdated to December 30, 1990, because Koskie wanted to get all the money out of his Communication Allowance before the end of the fiscal year. As with Gerald Muirhead's case, the police investigation started with a tip.

In the spring of 1993, a former employee with the Phoenix Advertising Group (a company that had strong ties to the NDP) tipped off a senior government employee that the company had paid a kickback to Koskie. From there, the matter was handed over to the RCMP. According to the statement that accompanied the RCMP search warrant, a Phoenix official alleged that there was an intention to write Koskie a cheque after getting money from the government and taking a 10 percent handling fee. The statement said police had conducted a search of documents at two locations and found a $1,250 cheque marked "donation" that the company had paid to Koskie.

Murray Koskie made his first court appearance in late December 1993. He was facing two counts of fraud over $1,000 and two counts of breach of trust. One of the fraud charges alleged that between March 1991 and May 5, 1991, Koskie submitted a false invoice for $1,250 for "communications consulting." The information filed with the court also alleged that Koskie failed to disclose that he received a refund of $1,250 related to the invoice. The other fraud charge alleged that he failed to disclose he received a $1,150 refund concerning another invoice for communications consulting. The breach of trust charges were connected with the two fraud charges and alleged that he used the $2,400 for his own personal purposes.

Because of a dispute about judges' salaries in the Legislature, the entire provincial court was disqualified from hearing Murray Koskie's preliminary inquiry, and his case proceeded to trial in Court of Queen's Bench by a direct indictment. The first thing Koskie's lawyer, Morris Bodnar, did was write to the justice minister with a request that the charges be dropped because his client had cancer. The request was turned down.

When Murray Koskie's trial began in late January 1995, Sergeant John Leitch laid out the Crown's case in two paper trails. The first trail began in 1989 when Koskie submitted an expense claim to the Legislative Assembly for work performed by the Phoenix Advertising Group. In the expense claim, Koskie asked the Legislature to pay Phoenix directly for consulting work done for him. A few weeks later, Phoenix deposited a government cheque for $1,465. Three days later, Phoenix wrote a cheque to Koskie for $1,150. The second paper trail began in March 1991. Koskie submitted a $1,250 claim for services that he received from Phoenix. The advertising firm deposited a government cheque for $1,250 the following month. Twenty days later, the company wrote a cheque to Koskie for $1,275.

Shelley Selinger, vice-president of Phoenix, testified in court that she did not feel "comfortable" giving money to Murray Koskie but followed his instructions anyhow. Selinger said Koskie contacted her in late 1990 because he was interested in sending a Christmas message to his constituents. Phoenix did not perform the work, but Selinger said Koskie told her to issue an invoice for $1,250. "I billed him and then later, Mr. Koskie came back to me and wanted his money back," she said. She said she put a cheque for $1,250 in the mail. She told the court that she later approached the company's accountant with her reservations. She said the accountant told her to call Koskie and tell him to return the cheque or destroy it, and Phoenix would issue a second cheque for a different amount and mark it "donation." She said the accountant said it would look fraudulent otherwise. A second cheque was issued for $1,275 and Koskie deposited it into his personal bank account.

Murray Koskie admitted he received the cheques from Phoenix and deposited one into his personal account and the other into his constituency account. He says the payments were political contributions. His lawyer accused Phoenix management (including the president of the company, Graham Baker) of covering up the real story in order to stay in favour with the NDP and preserve millions of dollars in government contracts. He argued that when company brass found out Koskie was seriously ill with cancer, they decided to give him the $1,250 as a political donation. Graham Baker told the court that he would have offered Koskie a political donation if he had requested one, but he did not recall making a donation as large as $1,250. He said he knew nothing about the $1,250 cheque. Court of Queen's Bench Justice Gene Maurice found Murray Koskie guilty on both counts of fraud. He stayed the breach of trust charges. Sentencing was delayed for about five weeks.

Over at the Legislature, Premier Roy Romanow began to get heat from the opposition parties for not kicking Murray Koskie out of the NDP caucus and the party. Romanow refused to comment on the case until Koskie was sentenced. Koskie had not been in the Legislature since he was charged. On the day of sentencing, March 11, 1995, Koskie was ordered to pay a $5,000 fine and to make restitution of $2,400 to the provincial government. The judge also sentenced him to a day in jail but deemed the time had been served by his appearances in court. Outside the courthouse, with his lawyer standing by his side, Koskie told reporters that he was innocent and said that he would appeal his conviction. He said that in the meantime, he would do the "honourable" thing and resign. He was eligible for an MLA pension of more than $51,000 a year. "It's a sad day, obviously, for Murray and his family," Premier Roy Romanow told reporters at the Legislature. "It's a sad day for the province." There was no doubt it was a dishonourable end to a twenty-year political career.

The public debate over the Murray Koskie case did not end there. Both opposition parties in the Legislature—the Liberals, who were the official opposition, and the Conservatives—questioned why Phoenix and some of its senior people were not charged with fraud. In an attempt to clear the air and to get the heat off them, the New Democrats hired an independent prosecutor from Calgary, in the neighbouring province of Alberta, to look at the case. The independent prosecutor concluded that the file had been handled properly and that there was "absolutely no substance to the suggestion that any political consideration may have influenced decisions made in the case." The Saskatchewan Court of Appeal threw out the conviction on one of the fraud charges against Murray Koskie but upheld the other. After receiving the decision, Koskie continued to maintain his innocence. "I'll go to my grave believing that and I can live with that, regardless of any outcome." The Supreme Court of Canada rejected his application to appeal.

The Tory Walls
Come Tumbling Down

John Scraba held the key not only to the safety deposit boxes full of $1,000 bills, but also to much of what went on in the caucus office. He did most of the work setting up the companies and running them, and the RCMP desperately wanted to talk with him. Scraba, however, was refusing to co-operate.

In the fall of 1991, about a month after he left his job at the Tory caucus, Scraba moved to Verona, a small community near Kingston, Ontario, where his wife was living. The couple was having problems and Scraba hoped that proximity would help them work them out. The RCMP kept tabs on Scraba after the move. Police officers called him at his wife's home and even dropped in on him every now and then. Scraba said that on one occasion they arrested him and kept him in custody overnight before releasing him.

When things did not work out with his wife, Scraba moved, first to Winnipeg and then to Edmonton, where he had friends and stood a better chance of finding a job. Back in the summer of 1991, when the Tories realized the RCMP were looking into business practices at their caucus office, they hired a lawyer for John Scraba. As the investigation progressed, however, the lawyer told Scraba that he would have to pay $5,000 to retain his services and that the final legal bill might run as high as $70,000. Scraba said he was broke and applied to legal aid instead. Bill MacIsaac of Regina was assigned to his case. Scraba said MacIsaac warned him that he could be facing up to seven years behind bars for his role in Project Fiddle and advised him to co-operate with the Crown. He gave his first statement to police in Edmonton in May 1993.

On July 4, 1994, almost three years after Project Fiddle was launched, the RCMP issued a news release stating that forty-five-year-old John Michael Scraba had been charged with one count of fraud over $1,000, one count of conspiracy to commit fraud, and possession of the proceeds of fraud, which included $240,000 in cash and a vehicle. At his first court appearance just over three weeks later, Scraba didn't enter a plea, electing instead to be tried by a judge and jury. A preliminary hearing was set for December 1994.

Although Scraba's statements to the RCMP were under close wraps, reporters were able to piece together some of the details from testimony he gave at Lorne McLaren's preliminary hearing and later at hearings for other MLAs charged with fraud. Scraba told the judge that the communications pool set up in early 1987 was soon generating a huge surplus, as more money was coming in than the caucus could find ways of spending. Scraba began storing $1,000 bills in a lock box he kept in a filing cabinet at his office at the Legislature. He later opened two safety deposit boxes at the Canadian Imperial Bank of Commerce (using the name Fred Peters), and moved the money there.

When Crown prosecutor Eric Neufeld asked Scraba at Lorne McLaren's preliminary hearing why he had opened the second safety deposit box, Scraba replied that it was to protect himself. He testified that he was told that with an election expected soon, the money could be used at any time. He said Conservative MLAs in "power positions" and some people in the premier's office had designs on the money. "The reason I had two boxes was for self-preservation," he explained. "If one boss had designs on the money and wanted to use it all, then I would have more for another superior." He said he opened the safety deposit boxes under the assumed name because his marriage was in trouble and he didn't want anyone snooping around his personal financial affairs to find the money. Scraba claimed it was just coincidence that the $90,000 that was discovered by police in one of the safety deposit boxes closely matched the amount he said he was promised for handling the

Communication Allowance pool and the numbered companies.

The RCMP were still building the case for Project Fiddle and were eager to obtain interviews and statements from other Tories. Several of them had retained Prince Albert lawyer Clyne Harradence, who was soon to become a veteran of the Tory fraud trials. The RCMP, in a letter to Harradence, named the people they wanted to talk with and explained why. The letter stated that only two members of the group, Sherwin Petersen and John Gerich, were suspects in the fraud scheme. The letter also stated that some of the Tories who had already been questioned by police were not co-operating fully, while others were refusing to be interviewed.

The police were convinced that the pooling scheme was set up to benefit the PC caucus, while another scheme was designed to benefit individual MLAs. They also believed that John Scraba had handed out plain white envelopes filled with $1,000 and $100 bills to a number of MLAs, and they wanted to ask everyone on the list whether they had ever received cash from John Scraba. The RCMP also had many questions about the numbered companies in the caucus office, although they admitted that the majority of MLAs who contributed to the central fund of advertising money were kept in the dark about how the money was used.

When John Scraba's preliminary hearing began in December 1994, Crown prosecutor Eric Neufeld subpoenaed all living members of the former Grant Devine government. Eleven of them hired lawyers and tried to have the subpoenas quashed so they wouldn't have to testify. Four of the eleven—John Britton, Grant Devine, Harold Martens, and Bill Neudorf—were sitting MLAs. The others (all former MLAs) were Eric Berntson, Ted Gleim, Ray Meiklejohn, Lloyd Muller, Sherwin Petersen, Arnold Tusa, and Jack Wolfe.

Six Tory MLAs had testified and Muller was up next, when his lawyer, Fred Kovach, requested an adjournment. Kovach argued that if Muller was a suspect in the case, by forcing him to testify, the Crown was denying him his right to remain silent. Lawyers representing other MLAs soon stepped forward with similar arguments. The preliminary hearing in provincial court was adjourned to give lawyers a chance to put their arguments before a justice with the Court of Queen's Bench. Amidst this legal wrangling, Scraba's legal aid lawyer, Bill MacIsaac, conceded the Crown had introduced enough evidence to send Scraba to trial on all four of the charges he faced. In an unusual move, Crown prosecutor Eric Neufeld turned down the offer of proceeding to trial.

When they went before Court of Queen's Bench Justice Gene Maurice, the MLAs' lawyers argued that their clients were being compelled to assist in the investigation because if they took the stand, they would have to answer questions from the Crown. The lawyers said that Neufeld's decision to turn down Scraba's request to go straight to trial showed the Crown was more interested in investigating witnesses than in presenting its case against Scraba. In the end, Justice Maurice ruled that the "pursuit of truth" took precedence over the applicant's right to remain silent and the hearing was allowed to continue. A disgusted Clyne Harradence stated the hearing was nothing more than "a fishing expedition."

The preliminary hearing resumed in January 1995 and by the time it was over, the Crown had called thirty-six of the thirty-seven surviving members of the Tory caucus from 1986 to 1991. The lone exception was Bob Pickering, who did not return from his winter holiday in the United States to testify. The other member of the Tory caucus, Walter Johnson, had been killed in a car accident the previous year. Some of the former politicians who had refused to give statements to the RCMP had to tell their stories for the first time in court; others who had given statements to the RCMP changed their stories once they sat in the witness box. Two former cabinet ministers, Joan Duncan and John Gerich, admitted for the first time that they had received cash from Scraba, having previously denied it.

Crown prosecutor Eric Neufeld had the same question for each of the MLAs as they filed through the witness box: "Did you ever receive cash from John Scraba?" Ten of the thirty-six former MLAs answered: "Yes." A few of them admitted that taking the money was illegal. Most of them insisted they used the money to pay legitimate expenses they had incurred performing their duties as elected members of the Legislature. Twenty-six of the members denied receiving cash from Scraba.

John Gerich, who was appointed to Grant Devine's cabinet in 1989, told the court he heard from another MLA that it was possible to get cash from John Scraba. Early in 1991, when he estimated he would have money left over in his Communication Allowance when the general election was called later that year, he asked Scraba to help him obtain the balance in his allowance so he could use it for political advertising during the campaign. Gerich said he made a claim on his Communication Allowance for $4,000. He received $3,491 and John Scraba kept the remainder as a service charge. Gerich said there was no intent to break the law.

Harry Baker told the court he received small amounts of cash from Scraba on one or possibly two occasions. He said the cash was reimbursement for postage and other expenses he paid for out of his own pocket. Sherwin Petersen said he received about $3,000 in cash from John Scraba to cover the cost of a computer, printer, and computer software his wife bought for his constituency office.

Lloyd Muller told the court he obtained $5,375 under false pretences by simply walking into John Scraba's office and telling him he needed money. With Scraba's assistance, he made two false claims on his Communication Allowance totalling $10,360. He said he split the money with Scraba fifty-fifty. According to his testimony, the invoice submitted with a Request for Payment in 1988 stated the claim was for a newsletter for his constituents, but there was no newsletter. A few days later Scraba called him into his office and gave him an envelope with cash in it. Muller said he repeated the process about five months later.

Beattie Martin, a former sports broadcaster with the Canadian Broadcasting Corporation, decided to use his Communication Allowance to pay for his membership at the Regina Golf Club (about $980) and his Saskatchewan Roughriders' season tickets (about $400). He also purchased a camera with money from his Communication Allowance so his assistants could take pictures of him at events. Martin said he would sign a blank Request for Payment form and a couple of days later, John Scraba would give him the cash. He acknowledged that Scraba had to file false invoices in order to get the money. Crown prosecutor Eric Neufeld argued that all the politicians who received cash got the money because false expense claims were submitted through their Communication Allowances.

Most of the Tories who were forced to sit in the witness box and be grilled by Neufeld said they were too busy with their own duties to concern themselves with day-to-day operations in the caucus office. They assumed caucus chair Lorne McLaren, along with the caucus whip and deputy whip, were watching over the caucus office. Caucus chair Lorne McLaren said 90 percent of his time was spent in the Legislative Assembly, meetings, or his constituency. "I was caucus chair in name only," he said during numerous interviews with reporters. He said that he was too busy being an MLA to have time to supervise the caucus office, and that the demands made on members' time in the Legislature is beyond the comprehension of the public.

Grant Devine told the court that he was involved in some strategic decisions about what advertising medium to use, but he never got involved in the administration of the communications fund. Former Deputy Premier Eric Berntson said he "had no idea about the actual administration or logistical functioning of the thing [the communications fund]." He said it was not something he concerned himself with. George McLeod, another former deputy premier, said he "wasn't aware of how caucus was doing any of its business."

When he left the courthouse after his preliminary hearing, John Scraba brushed past reporters and their microphones, ignoring a barrage of questions. Scraba's lawyer, Bill McIsaac, told reporters it was too early to say what would happen next. Speculation began to surface that Scraba, faced with spending time in prison, had decided to be more open with police in hopes it would mitigate his circumstances. Eric Neufeld wouldn't comment on whether they were talking about a deal with John Scraba in return for his co-operation.

The parade of witnesses forced to testify at John Scraba's preliminary hearing provided the RCMP with new leads in their investigation, and it was obvious that a number of people were getting very nervous. One of the fall-outs at the time was particularly tragic. Jack Wolfe was thirty-nine years old when he took a shotgun, held it to his head, and pulled the trigger. He left behind his pregnant wife, Gail, and three young children. Gail found her dead husband and his suicide note in the office of their veterinary clinic in the small town of Rockglen, Saskatchewan, on the morning of February 2, 1995. When he shot himself, Jack Wolfe was one of the former Tory MLAs under investigation by the RCMP as part of Project Fiddle.

Wolfe was elected in the rural riding that included his hometown of Rockglen in 1988. He was appointed to the cabinet the following year as associate minister of health. He was later given cabinet responsibilities for urban affairs and Saskatchewan housing.

The RCMP were investigating Jack Wolfe because of a computer he had received from the Tory caucus office when he was an MLA. The police thought that Wolfe had purchased his computer with money obtained using a false expense claim. According to documents collected by Sergeant John Leitch, the computer was purchased with $3,221 drawn from Wolfe's MLA Communication Allowance. The invoice for the purchase listed the computer as "radio advertisements and newsletters," and the purchase was done using one of the numbered companies John Scraba had set up in the PC caucus office.

Jack Wolfe told the RCMP that there was nothing dishonest about the way he obtained the computer. He said that someone in the PC caucus office told him shortly after he was elected that most MLAs were using computers in their constituency offices. He said he was given a computer from the office of a PC caucus researcher at the Legislature in Regina. He said that when he lost his seat in the 1991 provincial election, he took the computer home for his children to play with. (At the time, defeated and retired MLAs were allowed to keep the equipment from their constituency offices; the rules have since changed.) After the RCMP first questioned Wolfe about the computer, he packaged it up and sent it back to the PC caucus office. When he lost his seat, Jack Wolfe resumed full-time practice with his wife at their veterinary clinic in Rockglen.

Friends described Jack Wolfe as a quiet, generous man who wouldn't deliberately hurt anyone or do anything dishonest. According to Gail Wolfe, her husband became very depressed when police began asking him questions about the computer and what he knew about the goings-on in the PC caucus office when he was an MLA.

Gail Wolfe believed her husband's suicide was triggered by depression, and the depression was caused by the intense pressure he was under because of the RCMP investigation. She said that after he testified at the preliminary hearing for John Scraba, he was depressed because he felt police and the Crown prosecutor hadn't believed him. She said a few days later Wolfe's lawyer, Clyne Harradence, called and said the RCMP were going to charge him.

In his suicide note, Wolfe wrote that death would be a way to spare his family the pressure of the police investigation. Here is what he wrote:

Dearest Gail, Tricia, Katie, Steven:

My time has come to leave you. I love each and every one of you with all my heart and my only regret [is] that my time with you all and the new baby could not be longer. My love extends to my mother and father and my brothers and to your family Gail.

I love you all. I love you all too much to have you bear the pain of having my name and reputation destroyed because of the partisan political interest of others.

I did not do anything wrong other than trust others and for that people are hard at work trying to make a name for themselves while destroying others like me. I will spare you the detail and this suffering will pass.

Please cremate my remains.

Good Bye and God bless you all.

Jack.

Gail Wolfe would not comment on what her husband might have meant by "partisan political interests" but she said they both believed there was a lot of political pressure behind the police investigation. She said Wolfe became particularly distraught after Christmas 1994, when rumours of more charges against more PC MLAs began. At that point, John Scraba and Lorne McLaren were the only ones who had been charged.

"I think that was the last straw for Jack," Gail Wolfe said. "I think he was at the point where he was sort of on the edge of having a nervous breakdown over this whole thing." She said her husband had convinced himself that regardless of what he said or did, people would not believe he was innocent. She decided to go public after his death because she wanted to "tell Jack's side of the story."

The day before he committed suicide, Jack Wolfe wrote a thirteen-page letter to Harradence. On the cover page, he wrote, "Please find enclosed my recollection of my computer acquisition. Many thanks for your patience and understanding."

A couple of months later, Gail Wolfe, in a letter to Clyne Harradence, wrote about the events leading up to her husband's suicide. In her letter she told Harradence that the day before he killed himself, Wolfe came home for supper and told her that Harradence had telephoned to tell him that a police officer had called. Harradence relayed that the police didn't believe that Wolfe had told the truth at John Scraba's preliminary hearing, and that they were going to lay charges against him.

Harradence also told Wolfe he wanted him to write his computer memoirs. Gail wrote that after her husband received this news, he looked sad and distracted. Her letter continued, "I told him that it was okay, nothing like that really mattered, no matter what happened, that for our family and us and for our business it really wouldn't matter. He left and come home at about 10 PM with his computer memoirs written out for me to read. After that (about 11:00) I went to bed, and I guess he came back to the vet clinic to finish his work and to finish his life. I believe he felt so desperate to escape this situation, even though he'd done nothing intentionally wrong, that he chose to end his life."

Later in the letter, Gail Wolfe wrote, "I know that the ultimate responsibility for suicide lies with the one who chooses it, but I feel that the RCMP, by their actions, gave him a shove off that cliff. If they had given him hope that he could tell the truth and be believed, he would still be alive. They didn't give him that hope when they accused him of lying under oath."

In the letter to Harradence, Gail Wolfe said she wanted two things: to have the RCMP officially clear her husband's name, and to pursue damages through legal means if there was a reasonable chance of success. She ended the letter: "If I can help in any way in light of the other people also facing this witch hunt, I would like to do so." Of the public statement she wanted from the RCMP she wrote, "I feel quite strongly that the way this was dealt with by the RCMP, it may not be legally wrong, but I think it was morally wrong for them to put that much pressure on him." She didn't get a statement from the police clearing her husband of any wrongdoing and a lawsuit was never launched against the RCMP or the provincial justice department. Sergeant John Leitch denied the RCMP ever threatened to charge Jack Wolfe.

There were other former Tory MLAs and party supporters who questioned police tactics during the investigation. Some of them claimed that the two police officers dealing with Jack Wolfe had crossed the line between an investigation and harassment. They also alleged that there was political interference in the investigation. As an example, they cited a letter to the editor published in the local newspaper in Jack Wolfe's constituency in the summer of 1992, a year after the police investigation began. In a letter headed "Angry About the Mess," the NDP member who beat Jack Wolfe in the 1991 provincial election wrote: "The deeper we dig the more corruption and malfeasance we are finding. If more arrests and trials are indicated we shall continue to lay charges." A couple of years after Jack Wolfe killed himself, Gail Wolfe sold the veterinary clinic they had owned together and moved her family to Michigan.

The Courthouse Parade

As police officers continued to dig through the pile of documents seized from government offices, banks, accountants' offices, lawyers' offices, and private homes, more shady deals surfaced. It was slow going. Investigators with the RCMP's commercial crime division had thousands of documents to study and a limited number of officers to assign to the case. In bank records alone, officers had to sift through five years of PC caucus bank account documents, including statements, cancelled cheques, and deposit slips. On top of that, there were the thousands of claims that were submitted to the Legislative Assembly by the thirty-eight MLAs under various allowances, plus bank accounts for some of those who were being investigated.

On April 19, 1995, the RCMP issued a news release stating that three sitting Conservative members, William Neudorf, Harold Martens, and John Britton, had been charged with fraud. Neudorf was PC house leader and the critic for agriculture and food in the small but seasoned nine-member Conservative caucus. Martens was the finance critic, while Britton was the caucus whip and the critic for social services. Police documents alleged that the three politicians had submitted false expense claims to the Legislative Assembly Finance Office.

Allegations of a witch hunt began to circulate, especially among Tories, many of whom argued that much of what was happening was politically motivated. They said most of the charges involved the often-confusing guidelines for MLA allowances, and they argued that these were procedural matters that should have been dealt with over at the Legislature rather than in the courtroom. There were some Tories, however, who admitted that things had gone wrong in the caucus office and that money had been stolen, but they laid the blame for any illegal activity squarely on Lorne McLaren and John Scraba. The ruling NDP, for their part, denied any knowledge of a witch hunt, as did the police. The RCMP and the Crown pointed out that the case was in the paper trails put before the courts.

Neudorf, Martens, and Britton held a news conference the same afternoon the RCMP sent the news release to the media. Stern faced, the three MLAs sat at a table together facing television cameras and a group of reporters with pens and paper at the ready. The charges were big news, and all the media outlets in the city were in attendance. Bill Neudorf started off the press conference. He said the MLAs wanted to meet with the media to try to "combat the court of public opinion." When Neudorf stared into the television cameras to lay it on the line, it was obvious how angry he was. "I want to make it absolutely clear there was no intention of personal benefit from any of these transactions [charges]," he intoned. Harold Martens, a rancher, was calmer as he told the reporters, "While my faith in the justice department has been depleted, we must rely on it to clear us of these charges." In a prepared statement, the men said that they would not take part in any caucus responsibilities until the charges against them had been dealt with. Tory leader Bill Boyd questioned the timing of the charges "on the eve of an election." (A provincial election was expected within a year and a half.) The RCMP responded that the three men were charged as the result of the same investigation that led to charges against Lorne McLaren and John Scraba.

Scrummed by reporters in the hallway in front of his office at the Legislature, NDP Justice Minister Bob Mitchell said he had been told about the new charges the previous week. Mitchell shrugged off Tory comments about the timing of the charges. He said he was simply told about the charges and that was the NDP government's only involvement. Pressed by reporters, Mitchell said the charges had not been laid for political reasons and "anybody who says [that] is just deliberately misinforming you. There is no political interference at all, in any aspect of the investigation. The decision to lay charges or the timing of the charges, or anything." The reporters fired questions like gun shots as they sensed the justice minister was withholding information. Mitchell finally revealed that another eight former Conservative MLAs faced charges. Neither Mitchell nor the RCMP would say who they were, whether they had already been charged, or anything about the charges.

Later that day, reporters used their investigative skills and learned that Michael Hopfner, a former Tory caucus whip, had been charged with fraud. In a telephone conversation, Hopfner confirmed that an RCMP officer had come to his hotel in Lashburn on the afternoon of April 18 and charged him with fraud. "There is a witch hunt going on and I'm part of the witch hunt," Hopfner said, taking up the Tory refrain. His voice passed along the telephone line, through a small black wire attached to the telephone receiver with a suction cup and into a tape recorder, where it was recorded for later use on radio.

The following day, the RCMP released the names of the others charged. Four of them were former Tory cabinet ministers— John Gerich, Grant Hodgins, Lorne Kopelchuk, and Sherwin Petersen. Former caucus chair Harry Baker was also charged. The police said two others had been charged, but they would not release their names until they had been served with summonses to appear in court. The following week, the RCMP released the names: Joan Duncan and Ray Meiklejohn, both former cabinet ministers in Grant Devine's government. When he was contacted by a reporter, Meiklejohn said, "I certainly don't feel I've done anything wrong." Thirteen people had now been charged as the result of Project Fiddle.

Grant Devine, who up to now had been reluctant to talk to reporters about the police investigation, decided it was time to say something. The former premier, who was a sitting member of the Legislature, repeated the Tories' allegation that the police investigation was nothing more than a witch hunt driven by politics. Devine accused the NDP government of exploiting the situation in a pre-election ploy to discredit the Conservatives. "It's very sad to think that in good part, they're caught up in an attack on perhaps one or two individuals who may have made some serious mistakes—may have." Devine refused to name the one or two individuals, but it was obvious he was pointing the finger at Lorne McLaren and John Scraba. "But the rest," he said, "it's just very unfair and it makes me sad." When contacted by a reporter, Grant Hodgins was adamant he had done absolutely nothing wrong and that somebody was "over-anxious to make a name or there's somebody on some sort of crusade." Michael Hopfner agreed, "It's all politics and everybody wants to feed on the carcass, and we happen to be that carcass."

The eleven people who were charged in April 1995 made first court appearances on May 8. They sat together with their lawyers in a packed courtroom on the second floor of the provincial courthouse in downtown Regina. One by one, the court clerk read out the names. Two of them were given dates for preliminary hearings, and the rest of the cases were adjourned. Later, speaking with reporters on the sidewalk outside the courthouse, a still-angry Bill Neudorf said he was filled with "disbelief, total disbelief, sadness, and unhappiness" when he had to sit with his former colleagues in the courtroom. Grant Hodgins, seemingly unmoved by it all, told reporters, "The gentlemen and ladies that I served with are all fine, decent people and they are all good, honest, hard-working people, every one of them respected in their own communities. Every one of them elected by a majority of people in one or two or more elections." He concluded, "As for myself, I welcome the day I go to court and have an opportunity to clear my name."

The first of the group to go to trial was fifty-seven-year-old Lorne Kopelchuk. His trial began on September 18. Kopelchuk, a short man with a quick step, came to court dressed in a suit, tie, and overcoat. Before entering provincial politics, Kopelchuk had spent sixteen years working as the accountant-bookkeeper at a car dealership in the town of Canora, near the Manitoba border. He spent five years on the Canora town council, most of it as mayor. He was considered a pillar of the community, and he had a long history of community work. Kopelchuk was first elected to the Provincial Legislature in the 1986 general election. Three years later he was appointed minister of parks and renewable resources and minister of northern affairs. He was defeated in the next general election in 1991.

The RCMP alleged that while he was an MLA, Kopelchuk had used a false expense claim to draw $1,568 from his Communication Allowance. According to police documents, Kopelchuk failed to disclose that the money, which was obtained using an invoice for "audio presentation: speeches and material," had actually been used to pay for a portable, electronic public address system. The false expense claim was accompanied by an invoice from one of the numbered companies John Scraba had set up in the PC caucus office. Kopelchuk elected to be tried by judge alone.

RCMP Sergeant John Leitch laid out the Crown's case. He flipped charts, graphs, invoices, cancelled cheques, and government and bank documents on an overhead projector and displayed them on television monitors set up around the courtroom. During his testimony he constantly checked files in his laptop computer. According to his records, Lorne Kopelchuk was one of six MLAs who had used their Communication Allowances to purchase portable, electronic public address systems for $1,568 each in June 1988. Two others—John Gerich and Michael Hopfner—would eventually be charged. In an interview with a police officer during the investigation prior to charges being laid, Lorne Kopelchuk said he knew it was possible to cheat the system back in 1988. He said it was "shop talk" around the Legislature.

In his testimony at Kopelchuk's trial, John Scraba told the court a group of MLAs asked him to investigate portable, electronic public address systems complete with podiums. He says he checked out a few and then recommended one. Six of the MLAs decided to buy them. Scraba said he also arranged for the members to buy signs with their names engraved on them to attach to the podiums. After he was defeated in the 1991 general election, Lorne Kopelchuk kept his podium in his home in Canora. Over the next three years, he loaned it out to groups and organizations in his former constituency and then, in 1994, he donated it to the town of Canora.

Each public address system cost $940. When the taxes were added, the bill came to $1,005.80. Each MLA, however, was billed $1,567.55. John Scraba made a profit of $525 on each system.

Scraba said he was told to make a profit on the systems, but he couldn't remember who told him to do this. The $525 profit, he said, went to the PC caucus. John Scraba also told the judge that he got the public address systems for Kopelchuk and the others and charged them to their Communication Allowances at their request. He admitted using phony expense claims.

When it was Lorne Kopelchuk's turn in the witness box, he said he purchased the public address system after John Scraba told him that it was a good idea for a rural representative to have one. He told the court he didn't know Scraba had submitted a false expense claim for the system. "My intention was to purchase it through proper channels," he said, in response to a question from Crown prosecutor Eric Neufeld. "Isn't it true you got a podium paid out of public funds using a false expense claim?" Neufeld demanded at one point during the gruelling two-hour cross-examination. Despite objections from his lawyer, Orest Rosowsky, Kopelchuk replied, "At this time, yes. At that time, no." He said he "trusted Mr. Scraba" and he assumed the invoice would be made out for a podium when it was submitted. He said he never saw the invoice and he didn't question it being charged to his Communication Allowance. Kopelchuk told the judge he didn't fill out the false invoice, John Scraba did.

The clerk of the Legislative Assembly, Gwenn Ronyk, testified that the members' handbook clearly stated that a public address system was not an eligible expense for a member's Communication Allowance. She said that under the rules Kopelchuk and the others could have bought the systems by claiming the purchases under their Constituency Office and Services Allowances, which were to cover the costs of running members' constituency offices. Most MLAs, however, spent all or most of their Constituency Office and Services Allowances each month, while there was usually money left over in their Communication Allowances. MLAs could draw on their Communication Allowance at any time as long as they were within the maximum annual limit. The monthly claim on the Constituency Office and Services Allowances was limited to one-twelfth of the annual allowance.

In his final arguments to Provincial Court Judge Janet McMurtry, Orest Rosowsky argued that most people would not view a public address system as a piece of office equipment. It's used, he said, to communicate with constituents. He argued that John Scraba handled the transaction the way he did because it was just another way for him to make money by overcharging for the system. Rosowsky said his client was "a dupe" who had no idea a false invoice would be used to pay for the public address system, and that he couldn't be convicted for someone else's—in this case John Scraba's—criminal act.

Crown prosecutor Eric Neufeld argued that Kopelchuk knew the podium could not be bought legally with his Communication Allowance so "he turned a blind eye to the obvious" and never asked how the purchase would be made. He said Kopelchuk's explanation of what happened did not "hold water." Neufeld argued that "in either case, he is guilty of fraud." The judge promised a decision in a week.

"I am extremely relieved that the trial is over," Kopelchuk told reporters who were waiting outside the courthouse. "The stress part is [like] you wouldn't believe. I hope you never have to go through it because, on a personal basis, it's taxing and, without question, your family and your pocket book suffer immensely. You're taking on quite a system there. They have unlimited resources and it's hard. Going through these hallways with all these courtrooms, I sympathize with a lot of people that have to go through a lot of stress as they go through their trials or prelims [preliminary hearings] or whatever they happen to be going through. I really sympathize with some of those people that maybe had more serious charges than I did."

On September 28, Lorne Kopelchuk was acquitted. Judge McMurtry found that it was reasonable for him to have trusted a person of John Scraba's position within the caucus, and that there was no evidence that Kopelchuk knew that Scraba was likely to create or be a party to a misleading invoice. The judge accepted Kopelchuk's testimony that he didn't know that Scraba planned to misdescribe the public address system on the invoice. She even went so far as to say, "I do not see that a lectern is so obviously an office expense and not a communication expense that the submission of a lectern as a communication expense was, in itself, a dishonest act."

Kopelchuk was all smiles when he walked out of the courthouse and faced reporters. A reporter asked how he felt when the judge announced the decision. "I was numb," he replied. "I was set for a decision either way, and I just didn't really think, believe it or not. I tell you one thing. I didn't feel like going 'Whoopee.' It's just been too much of a nightmare for that. You don't recover from this." He said it was simple things that bothered him the most. "I was asked a year ago, before the charge was laid, when I was under investigation, . . . to be treasurer of my Church. I didn't tell them why, but I turned it down. I'll go through life remembering this one. It was a nightmare."

A little over a month after Kopelchuk's trial ended, on October 31, 1995, Crown prosecutor Eric Neufeld was back in provincial court in Regina with another former Tory cabinet minister. This time it was Grant Hodgins.

Grant Hodgins runs a family auction business in Melfort, in the heart of Saskatchewan's grain belt. His is a tall, heavy-set man with a thinning hairline who walks with an air of confidence. Hodgins was first elected as the MLA for the district of Melfort in the Conservative sweep in 1982. He was twenty-six at the time. He was first appointed to the cabinet in 1985. During his political career he held several portfolios: environment, public safety, and native affairs. He was also government house leader. He resigned abruptly in 1991 in a dispute over Grant Devine's controversial Fair Share Program.

Hodgins was charged with one count of fraud under $5,000. The RCMP alleged that he submitted a false expense claim for $3,645 through his Communication Allowance in September 1988. The police accused Hodgins of failing to disclose that the money was used to pay for computer software, which the MLA wanted for his constituency office. At the time, computer software was not listed as an acceptable item under either the Communication Allowance or the Constituency Office and Services Allowance.

As in Kopelchuk's case, the invoice that accompanied Grant Hodgins' Request for Payment was for "audio presentation and speeches," work that is allowed under the Communication Allowance. The invoice came from Images Consulting, one of the numbered companies John Scraba had set up in the PC caucus office. Hodgins was a member of the Board of Internal Economy—the all-party legislative committee that set the rules governing expense allowances—when the transaction occurred. He was, therefore, in a position to be well acquainted with the rules governing MLAs' expense claims.

The issue of whether computer software should be covered by one of the MLA allowances came up at a meeting of the Board of Internal Economy in December 1988. Hodgins made a motion that computer software be approved under the Communication Allowance—the fund he had used to purchase his computer software in September. Staff with the Department of Finance recommended that it come under the Constituency Office and Services Allowance instead. In the end, the board picked the Communication Allowance, and computer software was allowed retroactive to January 1988. Grant Hodgins had paid for his computer software on October 19, 1988.

"It's naturally a little unsettling," Hodgins said when his trial began in late October 1995, "but I am certainly looking forward to being completed with the process." He hired Melfort lawyer Stuart Eisner to argue his defence. When Grant Hodgins took the stand, he too blamed John Scraba. He told Provincial Court Judge Diane Morris that he didn't know Scraba was going to submit a false expense claim. Crown prosecutor Eric Neufeld argued that Hodgins went to Scraba when he found out the computer software could not be covered by his Communication Allowance. Scraba testified that he believed Hodgins knew a false invoice was being submitted on his behalf. The judge reserved her decision until December 15.

Meanwhile, John Scraba's case was continuing. There was speculation that he would be entering a guilty plea, but as he entered the courthouse on September 20 to testify at Lorne Kopelchuk's trial, he wouldn't confirm or deny the report. "It's part of the process," he said in response to questions from the reporters who were waiting for him. Scraba's lawyer, Bill MacIsaac, wouldn't comment on what they were going to do next.

"Guilty pleas are always possible" was all he offered. About a month and a half later, John Scraba struck a deal with the Crown. He agreed to plead guilty to a charge of defrauding the Government of Saskatchewan of over $837,000. In return, the Crown agreed to stay charges of conspiracy to commit fraud, and a charge of possession of $240,000 and a car obtained through a criminal offence.

Back in the courtroom once again on November 8, 1995, John Scraba stood with his hands clasped before him as the court clerk read out the details of the amended fraud charge. Court of Queen's Bench Justice Ted Noble then asked Scraba if he understood what was read to him. "Yes," he replied. Scraba was asked how he wanted to plead. "Guilty," he replied. Then he sat down. Scraba stared straight at Eric Neufeld as he summarized the evidence against him. The Crown prosecutor argued that Scraba's motive had been personal profit. To back up the argument, he referred to the letter Scraba had that showed he hoped to get a fee of 10 percent of all the money that flowed through the secret caucus companies. If everything had gone undetected, Scraba could have pocketed about $90,000, the same amount police found in one of the safety deposit boxes Scraba had opened in a Regina bank under an assumed name.

The RCMP first learned about the letter when Scraba testified at Lorne McLaren's preliminary hearing in 1994. At the time, the revelation took both the Crown prosecutor and the police by surprise. During testimony about the $90,000, John Scraba said it was part of the reward he was supposed to get some time down the road for handling the companies. Scraba said he was promised he would get the money if the Tories lost the government. He said he was told if they didn't lose, his next step would be to set up an advertising agency that would get business from one or more government departments. "So my reward would be down the road," he said. When police officers searched his home in Verona, the letter was in the shed at the back of the house.

When Scraba moved to Edmonton, he took the letter with him and kept it in his mother's house for safekeeping. When asked where in his mother's house, he said he couldn't remember.

When police officers went to his mother's home, they found the letter behind a picture hanging on the wall. Scraba's sister had told them where to find it.

The letter is dated June 15, 1988. John Scraba said he typed it, but he couldn't recall the date. He also said caucus chair Lorne McLaren was in his office when he signed the letter, but he couldn't remember that date either. McLaren acknowledged it was his signature on the letter, but denied any knowledge of the agreement. "I don't recall ever seeing that letter," he said.

Sergeant John Leitch said when he first saw the letter he believed it was genuine. But then he discovered that the MLA letterhead the agreement was typed on did not come into existence until February 1991, nearly three years after the letter was purportedly written. The left-hand margin, where McLaren's name was typed, was out of line with the body of the letter. There were other irregularities as well, all of which suggested McLaren's signature had been superimposed on the body of the letter.

John Scraba said that about a month before the general election was called in the fall of 1991, Lorne McLaren told him to hang on to the money in the safety deposit boxes until he heard from someone. He said he buried the safety deposit box keys in a ditch somewhere outside Regina before he left for Verona in the late fall of 1991, because he did not want them on him, and then he forgot where exactly he had buried them.

In his summary, Crown prosecutor Eric Neufeld said the former communications director was an essential part of a scheme committed by persons who had been elected to serve the public, not to steal from them. He noted that even though Scraba was not an elected official, he owed a duty to the public not to cheat them and not to be a party to cheating them. "He was the detail man," he said. "He was the man who made this particular scheme [work]. He made it work for as long as it did and as well as it did."

Eric Neufeld also told the judge that he wanted to be fair to the accused. He noted that John Scraba had been co-operative in the investigation and that he had provided three taped interviews with the police. He said Scraba did all this without any promise of leniency. He acknowledged that information provided by Scraba had allowed police to progress in their investigation. "He is not the sole key to the Crown's case because much of this [case] is documentation, but he certainly has been of great assistance to the investigation, and I don't deny that for a moment," Neufeld told the judge. Neufeld noted that there were ten other cases before the court, that John Scraba would have to be a witness in them, and that his evidence would certainly form an essential part of those cases.

Neufeld said Scraba deserved some consideration for entering a guilty plea instead of putting the court through the time and expense of a lengthy trial. He recommended that John Scraba be sentenced to three years in prison. He also asked the judge to order that Scraba pay some restitution. He said Scraba should have to pay back what the Crown had been able to prove he got as a benefit from his crime. That included the 1988 Pontiac Tempest, which was paid for by one of the numbered companies. Scraba bought the car, registered it in the company's name—582807 Saskatchewan Limited, also known as Images Consulting—and insured it with cheques drawn on the account of Images Consulting. The cheque for the car was registered with the company as "computer software" and the bill for the car insurance was recorded as "computer insurance." The total bill for the car and the insurance paid by the public purse was around $17,211. Although the PC caucus did not actually own the car, on August 21, 1991, Lorne McLaren signed a bill of sale transferring ownership of the car from the caucus company to Scraba for $100. As the director of communications in the caucus office, John Scraba got a few other perks as well. Scraba was given a cell phone as part of his job. He says there was an extra one lying around the caucus office, so he took it and gave it to his wife. One of the secret caucus companies paid both their cell phone bills.

When it was the defence's turn to address the judge, Scraba's lawyer said the MLAs that Scraba dealt with must have known what was going on. He said, "I don't think anyone, including Mr. Scraba, realized where this would go, what a cash cow it would become. The scheme," he said, "developed into a fraud."

Scraba's lawyer asked for a sentence that would be considerably less than the three years requested by the Crown "in view of his involvement, in view of his past life, his absence of a criminal record, and in view of his extensive co-operation with the authorities in the course of the investigation." He told the court that his client did not regard the $240,000 that was found in the safety deposit boxes as his own money. The judge accepted that and even commended Scraba for "resisting the clear temptation to abscond with all the money in the safety deposit boxes before it was eventually found." (When the trial ended and the $240,000 was no longer needed by the police as evidence, it was returned to the Government of Saskatchewan.)

John Scraba then addressed the judge. He stood in the prisoner's box, holding a written statement in his hands.

It is certainly with deep regret that I face you under these circumstances today. Regret for actions that have brought me here and of course for an uncertain future. I would like to thank the court for the opportunity to make these comments and would like to apologize to the people of Saskatchewan for my actions in these matters.

I know the court has an understanding of this case and hopefully of what is happening in terms of the broader picture relating to a number of past MLAs. And I would like to add that it was not long after I became aware of this investigation, which was during the provincial general election campaign in October of 1991, that it was made clear to me that I would be charged in this matter and [I] remained under that impression up until March of 1993. At that time, Sergeant Leitch contacted me in Edmonton, letting me know that they would proceed against me in short order if I was not prepared to co-operate, indicating that things would be easier on me if I did. Subsequently, I agreed to a lengthy interview in May of 1993. A second one quite some time later and a third this past summer.

Since agreeing to co-operate in this matter, I essentially put myself on the investigator's time clock in the hope of mitigating my own circumstances. From early 1992 to the end of 1994, waiting for the investigation, being arrested at my home in Ontario in September of 1992, and subsequently released, and providing statements, and also from my preliminary hearing at the beginning of this year up until now, waiting again for some kind of mitigation.

During my preliminary hearing I also consented to trial after approximately eight days but the Crown refused, wanting to examine all the MLAs it could, even though Mr. Neufeld had stated at Mr. McLaren's preliminary hearing just prior to mine, that he had never refused consent committal to trial before that [i.e., that he had never refused a request to proceed to trial]. Then I further waited while the Crown waited on other individual charges and if that would affect me more favourably.

However, even as I was giving a third statement to the police this past July, clarifying some matters that arose out of my preliminary hearing, the Crown was presenting my counsel with a ten-point list of its position. One, in my lawyer's opinion, essentially gave me no credit for the previous two and a half years of co-operation and which reflected a position not much better off than if I would have simply let the police proceed against me early in 1993. Therefore, I believe I have helped further the Crown's overall case having been told that without my evidence, no one else would have been charged initially, and would hope that the court would consider this.

This latest position of the Crown [the recommended three-year jail sentence] was just given to me the day before yesterday. I mention this timeline, Your Honour, since most of this whole affair would have been behind me now, instead of me having to face the gruelling road ahead respecting the others that are charged, plus waiting for my own trial sometime next year if I would have chosen that route, which might have lasted up to three months, based on the preliminary hearing. I feel that while all the others charged have been dealt with rather quickly, all of them this year, too much time has already gone by in my case because believe me, Your Honour, the stress of these four years has been taking its toll and it's certainly not over yet.

Scraba explained that while working in the caucus office, he developed "a bunker mentality," which meant that once the scheme was up and running, he did not stop to question what he was doing. He went on to say:

It is only after leaving that environment that the light goes on and you stop rationalizing to yourself. At the time, I did not question the MLAs' needs for cameras, lecterns and computer equipment. I rationalized it because this equipment I was told was to be used by the MLA in the constituency and was allowable in fact under the other allowance [the Constituency Allowance, not the Communication Allowance where the money usually came from]. In terms of the case, I was told they needed to recoup expenses and since I had been aware for many years previous, politicians often use cash for a variety of reasons, and for that portion involving the MLAs' individual requests, other than the pool money, I did not question it. And for my error in judgement and lack of personal responsibility, and wanting to be a team player, waiting my just reward at the end of it all, I deeply regret and do apologize for.

As you can appreciate, this has already had devastating effects on my life, personally and economically. I'm left with no assets other than the car and the realization that achieving any kind of reputable employment with companies in the fields that I have held in my life will be highly unlikely and extremely remote given the circumstances and my age. I hope Your Honour believes me when I say that after what I am going through I certainly will never even come close to allowing anything like this to ever happen again.

He concluded by pointing out that, other than the benefits raised in the trial, he returned most of the money to the Tory caucus in one form or other, and that $229,000 of the $837,000 had been spent on legitimate radio advertising. He hoped that the judge would take these facts into account when handing down his sentence. The judge said he would deliver the sentence at three that afternoon. Reporters were waiting when John Scraba walked through the courthouse doors.

"What message would you have for Lorne McLaren?"

"I'd just wish him the best of luck."

"You said you took directions from him," a reporter shot back.

"I'm taking responsibility for my own actions. Others will have their own justifications to deal with."

"Were you dealt with properly by the justice system? You said in your statement that this has dragged on for a long time."

"I might have done things differently, had I known the way it was going to end up."

"What do you mean by that?"

"Well, I just feel I could probably have had this whole affair behind me by now. I thought I would mitigate my circumstances by doing the actions that I did, and I'm of the opinion now that I didn't mitigate my circumstances to any great degree, and I should have probably done this a long time ago."

When the court resumed that afternoon, Justice Noble said it was clear John Scraba played a crucial role in one of the most serious frauds ever perpetrated on the provincial treasury by elected officials.

[That] the scheme for misusing and misappropriating public funds was put in place and carried out by some members of the Legislature and of the government caucus pretty well described the enormity of the crime itself. It is clear that while the accused was an important player in this scheme, he was neither the originator nor the authority behind it. Those credits appear to go to Mr. McLaren and the caucus committee appointed to set the scheme in motion. The Crown acknowledges that the accused was not the engine of the scheme but merely the driver. The accused admits his complicity but says he was acting on instructions from the caucus chair and on occasion from other MLAs. Members of that caucus came to him for help in dealing with their Communication Allowance provided by the Legislature.

John Scraba said he took orders from a committee of MLAs. He said Lorne McLaren, John Gerich, Michael Hopfner, and Sherwin Petersen came to his office shortly after the caucus meeting in Cypress Hills Provincial Park in early 1987 to talk with him about setting up the pooling system. He said they wanted to know whether it would be possible to set up a couple of numbered companies to facilitate the work. He said after some discussion it was decided that he should contact a lawyer to see whether it could be done. He said he got back to the MLAs after talking with a lawyer and was told to go ahead and set up a couple of companies. He said the lawyer who did the work for him had three numbered companies ready to go, so he took all three of them. He got another numbered company from the same lawyer at a later date and registered that one as his own company. Scraba said he prepared a report on the companies' activities for caucus chair Lorne McLaren, caucus whip John Gerich, and deputy whip Michael Hopfner at the end of each year. And he said the three MLAs always had access to the files for all the companies, including bank statements, and that the files were kept in his office.

Justice Noble said he could sympathize with Scraba, since his directions were coming from "very estimable people, judged by their electorate to be fit members of the Legislative Assembly." He went on to say that "one can easily, as he obviously did, get carried along with the activities of these people, simply because it may not have occurred to him at first [that] there were very serious questions to be asked about the legality of a scheme that such persons put into motion. That is not to say he should not have asked those questions. Of course, he should have. But it is perhaps not a total surprise that he did not question the motives of these elected public servants." The judge concluded that Scraba was acting on instructions from others. He described him as an instrument of Lorne McLaren and the PC caucus authority. But he also noted that it was always open for him to walk away once he saw that the scheme was indeed a misappropriation of tax money. The fact he did not made him culpable.

Justice Noble sentenced John Scraba to two years less a day and ordered him to pay the Government of Saskatchewan $12,000 as restitution for the 1988 Pontiac Tempest. The RCMP officer who was sitting in the courtroom to the left of the prisoner's box got up and approached Scraba, put him in handcuffs, and took him out of the courtroom. "I think the judge did as fair a ruling as he was allowed to do," Scraba said as he was led from the courthouse in handcuffs to a waiting police van.

That night Lorne McLaren watched the late-night television news from inside the Riverbend minimum-security prison in Prince Albert to find out what had happened to John Scraba. He was incensed by the suggestion that Scraba had been following his orders. "I was angry last night when I heard that," he stated the next day, raising his voice. "I wasn't the king pin that tells Scraba what to do with all this money and so on. [That's] absolutely false. Who told Scraba to do it, I would not know. Whether he did it on his own, I wouldn't know, but I sure as heck didn't."

John Scraba served his time at the provincial correctional centre just outside Regina. He was released to a Regina halfway house after serving four months. He was granted full parole four months later.

A Cold Tory Winter

In late November 1995, winter tossed its blanket over the sleeping prairie. People huddled in the warmth of their winter coats as they walked along streets decorated with coloured lights in downtown Regina. For most people, it was the season for good times, good friends, and family, but for some Tories and their families, there was to be little Christmas cheer. Seventy-one-year-old John Britton was among them as on November 27, 1995, it was his turn to sit before a judge. Britton faced two counts of fraud. He was charged with obtaining $3,500 in cash after making a false claim on his Communication Allowance and illegally receiving $2,300 to buy a video camera. Another former Tory MLA, John Gerich, made a brief court appearance the same day on two counts of fraud over $5,000 and one count of conspiracy to commit fraud.

John Britton is a soft-spoken man who was born, raised, and educated in Unity, a small farming community west of Saskatoon. Before entering provincial politics, he sat on the Unity town council for eight years. He spent thirty-two years with Imperial Oil, most of it in the bulk franchise business. Britton was retired when he was first elected as the member for the district of Wilkie in 1978. He was appointed deputy whip two years later. He became whip after 1991, when the Conservatives were sent to the official opposition seats by the NDP victory. He didn't run in the 1995 general election.

When John Britton sat in the witness box, he told Provincial Court Judge Bruce Henning that the $3,500 he received in cash from John Scraba was an advance to pay for a newsletter he was preparing for his constituency. Although the expense was allowable under the Communication Allowance, according to the rules, Britton should have gotten the money only after the work had been completed, and an invoice from the company that did the work should have accompanied the request. Instead, Britton said he signed a blank Request for Payment form and gave it to Scraba. The invoice that accompanied the Request for Payment that Scraba sent to the Legislative Assembly described the work as "audio/video presentation consultation: materials speeches." Like the other phony invoices, this one was from one of the numbered companies John Scraba set up in the PC caucus office. Britton said when the newsletter was produced, it cost him over $4,000.

When it was John Scraba's turn, he told the judge that when he received the $3,500 from the Finance Office, he put it in an envelope and gave it to Britton. There were three $1,000 bills in the envelope. Britton said he was shocked when he received cash, but he didn't ask any questions. He testified that when Scraba handed over the envelope, Scraba said he had done him a favour and a little gratuity was in order. Britton said he was not sure whether he left some money on the table or not. Later, when Judge Henning asked him about that, Britton replied, "It's a little foggy right now."

As for the video camera, Britton said he signed another blank Request for Payment form and trusted John Scraba to ensure it was handled properly. The invoice, again from one of the numbered caucus companies, stated "newsletters: constituents of Wilkie." The Request for Payment was processed through Britton's Communication Allowance, and Britton used the money to buy a camera. Video cameras are not allowable items under Communication Allowances, but are allowed under members' Constituency Office and Services Allowances. Like most MLAs, however, Britton usually used up his full office allowance. Again, Britton received cash from Scraba and again he didn't ask any questions. "I trusted the man," Britton said in court. "I had no reason not to trust him." John Scraba testified that the invoice was attached when Britton signed the Request for Payment form and it wasn't made out for a video camera.

John Britton had hired a crusty, grey-haired veteran of

court battles as his lawyer. Prince Albert lawyer Clyne Harradence had represented, or was still representing, several of the Tories who had been charged or who were being investigated by the RCMP. Whenever he got the chance, Harradence fingered Scraba as the man who pulled the wool over everyone's eyes and masterminded the fraud scheme. When Harradence questioned Scraba at John Britton's trial, he pushed Scraba hard. "I think it is rather obvious," Scraba shot back at one point when Harradence was trying to pin him down on whether the MLAs knew what he was up to in the caucus office.

John Britton had also bought a portable, electronic public address system, the same as the one purchased by Lorne Kopelchuk. But Britton did it properly, through the proper MLA allowance, the Constituency Office and Services Allowance. He still, however, bought it through John Scraba and paid $525 more than he would have paid if he had purchased it himself. Britton had also arranged with Scraba to get a public address system for Britton's wife, for her church group in Wilkie. She too, and of course indirectly the church group, paid the extra $525. Britton said when he left provincial politics in 1995 he turned the public address system and the camera he had purchased with his allowance money over to the Legislative Assembly, even though he didn't have to.

On November 30, 1995, the judge dismissed the two fraud charges against John Britton because he felt the former MLA had "no criminal intent." The judge also said he found it credible that Britton relied on John Scraba and trusted Scraba to do things properly. Commenting on the guidelines for allowances, Judge Henning said they were not all that clear or consistent. He said Britton might well just have been careless.

"I'm relieved," John Britton told the reporters who were waiting for him outside. "I think my faith in the justice system has gone up, and I think I had a very fair trial."

"How did you feel when the judge said not guilty?" a reporter asked.

"I guess it's pretty hard to say. Maybe [like] the first time you realized what Christmas was all about."

Through the media, Clyne Harradence challenged Crown prosecutor Eric Neufeld to take another look at his case in Project Fiddle because of what Harradence perceived as a credibility problem with one of his key witnesses, John Scraba. Harradence noted that two judges had not believed Scraba's testimony. Neufeld responded that each case was different.

Next up was former Tory cabinet minister Bill Neudorf. His trial began on December 4, 1995. Neudorf faced one fraud charge. The RCMP alleged that while he was an MLA, he had received $1,050 in cash after he submitted false expense claims under his Communication Allowance.

Neudorf, a tall man with a full crop of dark hair, was first elected in the constituency of Rosthern, a rural riding just north of Saskatoon, in 1986. He was appointed to the cabinet in 1989 as minister of social services and the minister responsible for the Saskatchewan Legal Aid Commission. On account of the charges laid against him, he didn't seek re-election in 1995. Before entering politics, Neudorf had taught high school for twenty-two years and like many MLAs, he had a long record of community work.

In a statement he gave to the police in 1992, Neudorf said he obtained the $1,050 from his MLA allowance in order to pay for twenty-four golf shirts and 144 baseball caps, even though the Legislative Assembly had earlier rejected a Request for Payment for the same items. In early 1988, Neudorf had submitted a claim for T-shirts, baseball caps, mugs, pens, letter openers, key chains, and rulers, all bearing his name and the name of his constituency. The claim was worth $2,112.99. The Legislature had agreed to pay for everything but the T-shirts and hats.

In the interview with police in 1992, Neudorf acknowledged that hats were not eligible communication expenditures, but he said he was disturbed by the decision not to pay for the items. In his way of thinking it made no difference whether you had a mug with your name on it or whether you had a baseball hat with your name on it. Neudorf said John Scraba overheard him comment on what had happened and asked him what was wrong. He said he explained his problem and Scraba told him there would be no problem getting the Legislature to pay for the T-shirts and hats. John Scraba prepared another expense claim form and Bill Neudorf signed it. The invoice prepared by Scraba stated the claim was for "newsletter, constituents of Rosthern." A short time later Scraba gave Neudorf a $1,000 bill and a $50 bill.

Bill Neudorf said he didn't see the Request for Payment form or the phony invoice that John Scraba submitted to the Legislature. He told Provincial Court Judge Harvie Allan he trusted John Scraba to handle things properly. Crown prosecutor Eric Neufeld argued that Neudorf knew exactly what Scraba was doing and if he didn't, a reasonable person would have figured out that what was happening was fraudulent.

There were contradictions between Neudorf's statement to police and documents Sergeant John Leitch introduced in court. In the statement, Neudorf said he had already paid for the hats and T-shirts out of his own pocket when Scraba submitted the phony Request for Payment. Leitch produced documents that showed the supplier was not paid until six months after Scraba submitted the invoice. The second contradiction involved the cost of the items. Neudorf told police the claim for $1,050 covered the value of the hats and T-shirts. The invoice from the supplier was for $953.83 and that's how much the supplier was paid for the items.

Clyne Harradence, as he had done in John Britton's trial, put the blame squarely on John Scraba's shoulders. When it was his turn to cross-examine Scraba, he tried to portray him as a schemer who used people who trusted him. The judge reserved his decision until after Christmas.

The fraud trial for Harold Martens began on December 11. Martens was trying to fend off two fraud charges. On one charge, he was accused of using two false expense claims under his Communication Allowance to get $3,600 to buy a computer, which is an ineligible item under that fund. One claim was for $3,100; the other one was for $500. The invoices that accompanied his Request for Payment forms were for "newsletters for his constituency, the constituents of Morse, and for photo distribution." The invoices came from two of the numbered companies John Scraba had set up in the PC caucus office. The second charge involved $2,250. On this one, Martens was accused of using a false expense claim to get money from his Communication Allowance to buy a video camera, another ineligible item. The invoice, which also came from one of the numbered companies in the PC caucus office, was for "video presentation, consultation and materials."

When he was not actively involved in politics, Harold Martens, a big man who had an obvious dislike for reporters, operated a cattle ranch in the Swift Current area, in southwestern Saskatchewan. In 1977, he had been awarded the Queen's Silver Jubilee Medal for his contribution to local government. He was first elected as the member for the constituency of Morse in 1982. He was appointed to the cabinet in 1989 as associate minister of agriculture and food. He also served as the minister responsible for the Saskatchewan Water Corporation, Agricultural Credit Corporation of Saskatchewan, and the Saskatchewan Horse Racing Commission. He did not seek re-election in 1995.

Once again, Crown prosecutor Eric Neufeld and defence lawyer Clyne Harradence faced off in court. Neufeld argued that the evidence presented by RCMP Sergeant John Leitch and other Crown witnesses left no doubt that Harold Martens had participated in a fraudulent scheme. He also said it strained belief that a veteran MLA like Martens wouldn't know computers and video cameras were office expenses and not communication expenses. He argued that Martens "turned a blind eye." He said Martens "was reckless at the very least if he didn't know."

When it was his turn, Clyne Harradence described Harold Martens as an honest and respected member of his community who should be believed when he said that he had no knowledge of any fraudulent schemes and that he trusted his staff to make sure his expenses were handled properly. In this trial, as in previous ones, John Scraba was portrayed as the scam artist who set up the fraud scheme and took everyone for a ride. "I wasn't leading these people through the Red Sea and they were blindly following me," Scraba shot back in response to one of

Harradence's questions. At another point during his cross-examination, Clyne Harradence described Scraba as a "confidence man." He said that to find Harold Martens guilty on the evidence of "that rogue, that charlatan, that confessed thief, would be a very grave concern." Harold Marten's trial lasted four days. The judge promised a decision on February 15, 1996, a month and a half down the road.

The same afternoon Harold Martens' trial ended, December 15, Grant Hodgins was back in court. He was found guilty as charged. In her ruling, Provincial Court Judge Diane Morris said she did not believe Hodgins when he testified that John Scraba had submitted a bogus invoice to the Legislature without his knowledge or consent. She stated, "I am satisfied that Mr. Hodgins had full knowledge of what Mr. Scraba was going to do on his behalf, that he directed Mr. Scraba to do it, and that he intentionally participated in the deceit perpetrated to make an illegitimate claim which in the end deprived the public of its moneys." John Scraba got a mention as well. "Mr. Scraba had been involved in an elaborate scheme which enriched himself as well as others by submitting disguised claims for payment, taking a cut, and reimbursing certain members of the Legislative Assembly in cash and otherwise." Sentencing was put off for a month so a pre-sentence report could be prepared.

"I'd like to reserve a lot of my comments until sentencing," Grant Hodgins said as he faced reporters in the same controlled manner he had used for years as a politician when an issue was on the line. "It's naturally not the position I was looking for, but this is the day in court and I certainly respect this system."

"The judge obviously said he didn't believe your testimony. How do you feel about that?" a reporter asked.

"I think the whole tone of this entire case will be much more clear when we see what the judge decides in her sentencing decision, and at that time I think I'll have a little more comment on your question."

"You pleaded not guilty. Do you stand by that?" another reporter asked.

"My opinion is that I was not guilty of fraud."

"Do you still feel that way?"

"Absolutely."

"Were you surprised by the decision?"

"Yes, frankly, I was quite surprised."

In court, Grant Hodgins' lawyer had argued that his client's auction business required that he be bonded so he could travel, and that a criminal record would interfere with his ability to run the business. He said that a conditional discharge, which would mean no criminal record, would allow him to continue as president of Hodgins Auctioneers.

On January 15, 1996, a month after Grant Hodgins was found guilty, Bill Neudorf received a verdict of not guilty. His wife and one of his sons were in court with him when Provincial Court Judge Harvie Allan announced his decision. Judge Allan found Neudorf to be an unwitting participant in a fraud perpetrated by John Scraba. He said it would be easy, in an age of cynicism toward politicians, to assume Neudorf had turned a blind eye to the fraud, but he said the evidence suggested otherwise. He called Neudorf "naïve, unsophisticated, and guileless."

"Obviously I'm relieved. I'm happy but I'm standing before you with a lot of mixed emotions," Neudorf told reporters. When asked how he felt about the judge describing him as naïve, he replied, "I'd rather be naive and stupid than guilty. I have to admit I am filled with a certain degree of bitterness at the same time about what we have been put through. The last four years has been pure hell for my family, my friends, and myself." He said his political career had been shot down in flames. Neudorf, who had turned fifty-six a few weeks earlier, told reporters there would always be those who thought he did something wrong. As for politics, he didn't rule out getting involved again in some fashion down the road.

Bill Neudorf was the third former Tory MLA to be cleared of charges of defrauding taxpayers. Three others—Lorne McLaren, John Scraba, and Grant Hodgins—had been convicted. Sherwin Petersen, a former minister of highways, who was also facing fraud charges, sat in the courtroom when Bill Neudorf was acquitted. Petersen's preliminary hearing was to start later that day.

When Neudorf was acquitted, Ray Meiklejohn's case was working its way through the court. Meiklejohn's trial had begun on December 18, 1995. He had been charged with receiving $4,520 in cash after he submitted a false expense claim to the Legislature while he was serving as education minister. According to bank records seized by the RCMP, Meiklejohn deposited $4,500 in cash into his personal account six days after he received the money from John Scraba. Meiklejohn admitted receiving the cash, but he said he used it to purchase a computer and printer for his constituency office in Saskatoon. He told police he didn't know Scraba used a false invoice in order to obtain the cash on his behalf. The invoice was for "newsletters."

Meiklejohn was a public servant for most of his working life, first as a schoolteacher, then as a school principal, and subsequently, as a superintendent of schools. He was first elected in a Saskatoon constituency in 1986. Shortly after the election, he was appointed minister of science and technology, responsible for the Saskatchewan Research Council. In the following years, he was given cabinet responsibilities for consumer and commercial affairs and then education. He lost his seat for the constituency of Saskatoon River Heights in the 1991 general election.

In the courtroom, Ray Meiklejohn and his lawyer, Orest Rosowsky, who had successfully defended Lorne Kopelchuk, pointed the finger of blame at John Scraba, a tactic that appeared to have worked in the Kopelchuk case. Meiklejohn said he trusted the caucus communications director to handle the expense claim properly and legally. Crown prosecutor Eric Neufeld went for the "blind eye" argument again. He said that the transaction was so unusual that Meiklejohn "either knew exactly what was going on or at least turned a blind eye." He argued that Meiklejohn must have known something was amiss when Scraba handed him an envelope containing four $1,000 bills and five $100 bills. After hearing all the evidence, Provincial Court Judge Ross Moxley reserved his decision until

January 25, a little over a month away.

On January 19, 1996, Grant Hodgins was back in court for sentencing. He was handed a conditional discharge, which meant that if he kept the peace and abided by the conditions laid down by the judge, he would not have a criminal record. In her reasons for granting the conditional discharge, Provincial Court Judge Diane Morris said she had considered the fact that Hodgins had no previous criminal record and was not likely to re-offend. She agreed with the defence argument that a criminal record might hurt Hodgins' ability to run his auction business. She ordered Hodgins to pay restitution of $3,645, the exact amount he had received using a false expense claim to buy computer software, and she ordered him to do 240 hours of community work before the end of the year.

"Just like old times," Grant Hodgins said as he approached reporters outside the courthouse. Once again he presented a professional and polished image. "I'm pleased that the judge chose to look at all the different circumstances and grant me a conditional discharge, which will mean no criminal record. To me personally," he said, "that is very important, and to the people I work with, fifteen or so families, to their employment, it is also important." Grant Hodgins continued to maintain he had done nothing wrong. "I want to be very clear that I feel that what I did was not wrong," he told reporters. "For forty years I've tried to be straight and honest in every way. It's very, very hurtful that record has been blemished." He said he just wanted to get on with his life and he was going to chalk this one up as a "bad experience."

When Ray Meiklejohn faced Judge Moxley again on January 25, he was found guilty as charged. After summarizing the evidence against the former Tory education minister, the judge said, "In short, I find that by virtue of Meiklejohn's wilful blindness, the necessary mental element has been proven beyond a reasonable doubt." The judge also noted that the other elements of the charge were proven beyond a reasonable doubt. This was the first time a judge had accepted the Crown's argument that at least some Tories knew something was wrong in the caucus office but "turned a blind eye."

Meiklejohn was given a conditional discharge, put on probation for a year, told to do 240 hours of community service work, and ordered to pay back the $4,520 he received by submitting the phony expense claim.

Outside, on the courthouse steps, a devastated Ray Meiklejohn told reporters, "Obviously I'm very disappointed. That is not what I had expected at all, but I am glad that it is over. I appreciated the fact [the judge] said in his comments that there was no personal gain on my part and that I also knew nothing about the scam that was going on with Mr. Scraba. I certainly do not feel that I have done anything wrong. I was maybe trusting the wrong people. Maybe there are questions that I should have asked that weren't asked. So be it."

"Did you turn a blind eye?" a reporter asked.

"No, I did not turn a blind eye. Mr. Scraba was in a position of trust and anytime you are a minister, or in a business, or in a position where you have a lot of duties to perform—and I was in charge of two departments at the time—you have to rely on other people, and I was relying on Mr. Scraba. When the director of communication suggests to you that this is something that can be done in a legal manner, why would I question him?"

Meiklejohn said he expected his business would be affected by the verdict. He worked for an insurance company selling registered savings plans to parents for their children's education. He thought there would be people who felt he was guilty. Meiklejohn said he would always look back on his years in politics as a good experience, even though the trial had put a "black mark" on it.

Harold Martens was back before a judge for a decision in his case on February 15, 1996. Provincial Court Judge Leslie Halliday found him guilty of intentionally using deceptive means to obtain a computer and a video camera. The angry fifty-four-year-old rancher uttered a terse "no comment" when reporters approached him as he left the courthouse. In contrast, his lawyer, Clyne Harradence, was eager to talk. He told reporters that his client was devastated by the conviction. "He hadn't had a speeding ticket," he said facing the television cameras on the sidewalk after Martens had driven away in a pickup truck. "He is a respected man in his community."

Harold Martens' case was Harradence's first loss after helping three Tories beat fraud charges. A month later Martens was granted a conditional discharge. He was put on probation for a year. He was also ordered to repay $5,850, the money he illegally received to buy the computer and video camera, and to perform 240 hours of community service work. Martens was the fifth Tory to be convicted of fraud as the result of Project Fiddle; three others had been acquitted.

Michael Hopfner's Soap

"Well, it's just unbelievable. I guess we just carry on. It's like living in hell." That was Michael Hopfner's response after a judge ordered him to stand trial for fraud. It was February 14, 1996, a few days short of ten months since he had been charged in connection with Project Fiddle.

The forty-nine-year-old former Tory MLA, a tall, thin, serious-looking man, was an electrician by trade, but he had been dabbling in business and politics for years. He was an electrical contractor for a while, the director of the province's hotel association, and for a few years he was the mayor of Lashburn, a small town in west-central Saskatchewan. At the time he was charged, he owned a hotel in that town.

Michael Hopfner was elected as the MLA for Cut Knife–Lloydminster in Grant Devine's big sweep in 1982. He was re-elected in 1986. In the late 1980s he served as the government whip and he was on the public accounts and special regulations committees. He lost his seat in the 1991 provincial election.

Now, the soft-spoken hotel owner found that he was in a lot of trouble. He had been fingered as one of the top guns in the Tory fraud scandal. He had worked in the caucus office, first as deputy whip and then as whip, during the time John Scraba filled out all those false expense claims and handed out thousands of dollars in cash to MLAs. The RCMP suspected that Hopfner had pocketed a good chunk of that money. They also suspected that he had helped to mastermind the whole scheme to defraud taxpayers of more than $837,000. As deputy whip and whip, Hopfner had signing authority on the caucus account, and he was one of the big bosses in the caucus office, at least on paper.

As Michael Hopfner waited for his trial, Crown prosecutor

Eric Neufeld moved on to other Tory fraud cases. On April 11, 1996, former Tory cabinet minister Joan Duncan pleaded guilty to defrauding taxpayers of $12,405. Duncan was first elected as the MLA for Maple Creek, located in the southwest corner of the province, in 1982. During her time in government, she held the portfolios for economic development and tourism, revenue, and consumer affairs. Duncan had called off her preliminary inquiry the previous November after only two Crown witnesses had testified.

According to Sergeant John Leitch, Duncan received $12,405 in cash after submitting false expense claims under her Communication Allowance. At the preliminary hearing for John Scraba two years earlier, Duncan had testified that she received a $1,500 kickback and then flew to Hawaii, where she spent the money on clothes, souvenirs, and knickknacks. She said she took the money in a fit of anger after being dumped from Grant Devine's cabinet in the fall of 1989.

Duncan told the court that she had felt betrayed because after being a team player throughout her political career, her reward was a kick in the mouth. She considered resigning her seat on the spot. She said she told John Scraba that she would not be putting any more of her Communication Allowance into the caucus central pool. She said Scraba asked her how much she wanted. She told him $1,500 would do it. She filled out a Communication Allowance request form for $4,995, and Scraba gave her an envelope containing $1,500 a few days later.

When the RCMP interviewed Joan Duncan in October 1992 and again in September 1993, she denied ever accepting cash from John Scraba. When asked why she changed her story at Scraba's hearing, Duncan replied, "It's a matter of living with your conscience for this many years. Something that was so stupid, such a stupid thing to do, and to do it in a fit of anger and then come to the realization it could actually destroy your reputation." She said she was relieved to have finally told the truth.

At Duncan's trial, Sergeant John Leitch produced documents that alleged she had defrauded the government with phony claims on three different occasions, totalling $12,405. Although Duncan pleaded guilty to all the allegations, she insisted that she received only $1,500 in cash from John Scraba. She said she accepted responsibility for the total amount because of her "wilful blindness." Duncan admitted signing two false expense claims worth $10,905 on two other occasions before she left politics in 1991, but said the proceeds went to the PC caucus.

At her sentencing hearing on May 11, 1996, the fifty-five-year-old former cabinet minister, the only woman charged in Project Fiddle, sat silently and alone in the front row of the court bleachers while her lawyer, Fred Kovach, and Crown prosecutor Eric Neufeld presented arguments as to why she should or should not be sent to jail.

When she came back for sentencing on May 28, Joan Duncan gave a brief statement to the court saying she was sorry for what happened. She told Provincial Court Judge Ken Bellerose that her biggest regret was for her four children. She had raised them to be honest and after what she had done, "sometimes it's a little hard to face them and reinforce that." In handing down the sentence, the judge told Duncan he would have sent her to jail if the Crown had appealed any of the sentences given the other MLAs who had been convicted of fraud. Most of them had been given conditional discharges, which meant they would not have criminal records after following the judges' orders for probation and community work.

Judge Bellerose said the defence request for a conditional discharge in her case was totally out of the question. He suggested that a discharge would create a crisis in confidence in the administration of justice. He didn't stop there. He noted that the Court of Appeal had stated that a custodial sentence is traditionally required when a person in authority abuses his or her position of trust. He went on to say that welfare recipients have gone to jail for defrauding the government and farmers have gone to jail for defrauding crop insurance. He wondered why Duncan should be treated any differently. He stated that Duncan's crime was more "heinous" than welfare fraud, since she didn't take the money out of necessity. He also said that although Duncan deserved a six-month jail sentence, it would be unfair to single her out for incarceration, considering the sentences that had been handed the other former politicians who had been convicted of fraud. When Crown prosecutor Eric Neufeld was asked why the Crown had not appealed any of those sentences, he replied that those decisions were made at a more senior level. Duncan was fined $5,000, placed on probation for a year, and ordered to pay back $12,405. When they left the courthouse, neither Joan Duncan nor her lawyer would talk to reporters.

In the fall of 1996 the chief investigator for Project Fiddle, Sergeant John Leitch, was transferred from the force's commercial crime unit to the drug section. Some Tories had accused Leitch of being on a mission and said that he had won his sergeant stripes along the way. His boss, however, said it was a routine transfer and had nothing to do with his work on the Tory fraud investigation. Leitch would continue to be a key witness in the cases still before the courts and in any new cases that might come up.

Over at the Legislature, some NDP MLAs were talking about going after the Tories who had been convicted to force them to pay back the money they had stolen. On May 28, 1996, the all-party Board of Internal Economy, in a unanimous vote, decided to hire a lawyer to find out whether it would be worth suing the MLAs and workers who had been convicted of fraud. A lawyer in Calgary was hired. In his report released in December, Robert Thompson said there was a good chance that some of the money could be recovered through civil action. A Saskatoon lawyer was hired to launch the lawsuits. Four months later, the Saskatoon lawyer told the board it was a waste of time. Tom Gauley said there was "almost no chance" of recovering public money through lawsuits, so the Board of Internal Economy dropped the idea.

Meanwhile, the court cases continued. Michael Hopfner's trial began on September 3, 1996, a delay of nearly eighteen months since the date he had originally been charged. First he elected to be tried by a judge and jury, but by the time he showed up for his trial, he had changed his mind and announced that he wanted to be tried by a judge alone. He also announced that he would handle his own defence. He had acted as his own lawyer during his preliminary hearing six months earlier. He had lost there, but he hoped to do better now that he had some court-room experience. He had applied for legal aid but had been turned down because he had too many assets and he made too much money. He even went to court to try to convince a judge to order the province pick up the tab for his legal bill. When that failed, he tried to get the Saskatchewan Court of Appeal to consider his case, but the court wouldn't even hear his arguments.

Hopfner faced two counts of fraud over $5,000 and one count of conspiracy to commit fraud. He was accused of defrauding the government of over $837,000 and for allegedly helping set up and operate the scheme to get money illegally from the MLAs' Communication Allowances. The police also alleged he personally obtained $57,348 in cash using false expense claims. Hopfner deposited twenty-five $1,000 bills into his bank account during the period in which he was believed to have been submitting fraudulent expense claims to the Legislature. On one occasion in 1991, he deposited four $1,000 bills with serial numbers that were in sequence with other $1,000 bills found in one of the safety deposit boxes opened by John Scraba. Hopfner was accused of obtaining $42,448 using false invoices supplied by John Scraba and another $14,900 using false invoices that were supplied by another caucus employee, Michael McCafferty, who was a speechwriter in the caucus office when Hopfner was there.

Hopfner explained to reporters why he changed his mind and elected to be tried by judge: "There's a lot of people out there who . . . would just love to stick it to a politician." As if to confirm Hopfner's decision, one man who left the courthouse after being dismissed as a potential juror offered the opinion that politicians "should be shot." Michael Hopfner also explained why he didn't want to hire a lawyer. He said he had watched Lorne McLaren and others spend thousands of dollars in legal fees and he felt a lawyer would bleed him dry. And then, if he lost, there might be an appeal and yet more legal bills to pay. "It costs a lot of money," he explained. "Why should a person have to spend that kind of money if he didn't do anything? That's the way I look at it. I feel that people shouldn't have to spend a fortune, if they didn't do anything." Hopfner figured that a lawyer would cost about $1,000 a day and his trial might last as long as three weeks. To get that kind of money, he would have to sell everything he owned. That, he said, would mean putting his family out on the street and he'd sooner go to jail than do that.

In preparing for the trial, Michael Hopfner got help from a few friends who believed he was innocent. He set up his law office at a friend's house in a residential neighbourhood in Regina. There he studied the piles of documents the police and the Crown prosecutor were going to use to try to convict him.

When the trial began, it soon became obvious that Michael Hopfner was out of his league and in serious trouble. Court of Queen's Bench Justice Ross Wimmer was patient. He corrected Hopfner when correction was needed and guided him in his questioning and the finer points of law when he thought it might be helpful. It was clear, however, that the courtroom arena was quite a struggle for Hopfner, who was obviously more at home behind the front desk of his hotel in a small prairie town.

Crown prosecutor Eric Neufeld, with tons of courtroom experience behind him and a good grasp of Project Fiddle, laid out the Crown's case. By now, Sergeant John Leitch could tell the tale in his sleep. As in previous trials, Leitch and Neufeld used a slide projector, television monitors, laptop computers, and stacks of files to put their case before the judge. The document trail was similar to the ones used at other trials, with a few twists and turns thrown in with Michael Hopfner's name on them. According to Leitch, Hopfner had used false expense claims with the help of John Scraba to get cash. And, as with the other cases, the money came out of the MLA's Communication Allowance and was laundered through the PC caucus bank account.

When he testified for the Crown, John Scraba told the court that a small group of MLAs, including Michael Hopfner, oversaw the day-to-day implementation of the money pooling system. He also said that he filled out false expense claims for Hopfner and gave the former MLA cash. The false expense claims were funnelled through one of the numbered companies Scraba had set up in the caucus office.

When it was his turn to question Scraba, Hopfner spent nearly a day trying to poke holes in the former communications director's testimony. It turned out to be one of the more frustrating days for the courtroom rookie. He was interrupted on several occasions by Justice Wimmer as the judge wondered out loud about some of Hopfner's questions. "It's just not very clear to me what you're trying to get at," Justice Wimmer interjected at one point.

When Joan Woulds testified, she sided with Scraba and identified Hopfner as one of the MLAs who orchestrated the plan for the caucus communications pool, including the numbered companies. But it was clear Woulds also felt she had been used by Scraba.

Hopfner's trial was the first time anyone heard the details of how another caucus employee filled out false expense claims for two members—one of them being Michael Hopfner—and kept a share of the cash for himself. Michael McCafferty, who was a researcher in the caucus office and wrote speeches for the premier's wife, Chantal Devine, admitted to conspiring with Michael Hopfner and another MLA "to defraud the taxpayers of this province."

When McCafferty testified in response to Crown prosecutor Eric Neufeld's questions, he told the court that in early 1986, he needed money and asked Hopfner if he could help him. He said over the next few years, he and Hopfner submitted expense allowance claims worth several thousand dollars and divided the proceeds between them. He said the false invoices were usually for writing speeches and newsletters, but the work was never done. Hopfner admitted to having received money from Michael McCafferty, but he said it was repayment for money he had given McCafferty to do work for him.

When the Crown had put the finishing touches on its case, it was Hopfner's turn. After getting a few pointers from Justice Wimmer on how to handle his case, Hopfner turned to his witness list. As he laid out his defence, the doors to the Tory closets opened and more tales from the backrooms spilled out. Hopfner's witness list contained the names of most of his former colleagues in the Tory caucus. Police officers had no trouble serving subpoenas on his former colleagues, that is, all but Senator Eric Berntson, the former deputy premier. The problem was that police officers are not allowed to serve a subpoena on Parliament Hill, so they had to catch up with the senator somewhere else.

Hopfner was determined to get the senator into the witness box. "He seems to be able to push the buttons around the caucus, around the building," he said. "Maybe he knows something that I don't know." A young woman who was helping Hopfner made numerous attempts to contact the senator at his office and home in Ottawa. None of her calls were returned nor could she manage to track down Berntson.

Berntson's lawyer, Clyne Harradence, wrote a letter to the court complaining about Hopfner's attempts to get the senator to testify at his trial. Harradence expressed concerns about alleged threats made by the young woman who was doing the telephoning. In the letter, he also complained that an unnamed RCMP inspector had warned the Senate law clerk that if Berntson didn't voluntarily contact police, they would publicize that he was avoiding the subpoena. Harradence accused the police of trying to intimidate a witness, and he denied that Berntson was dodging the RCMP. The Senate clerk wouldn't comment on the letter or the alleged threat.

Along with the letter, Clyne Harradence also sent a copy of an opinion written by the Senate's law clerk. The opinion stated that one of the privileges of a senator is that of not being required to attend as a witness. The opinion cited another authority, which stated the immunity applies while the Senate is sitting and forty days before and after. The Senate had resumed sitting the previous Tuesday.

According to Joseph Maingot, a former House of Commons law clerk and author of a book on parliamentary privilege in Canada, MPs and senators are not required to appear as witnesses while Parliament is in session and technically speaking, Parliament is in session 365 days a year. The only open time, according to Maingot, is following an election call, when Parliament is dissolved until the government opens a new session. Maingot said one of the original reasons for this parliamentary privilege was to keep members of the British Commons from being hauled away to debtors' court during the eighteenth century. He also said the reason they couldn't be compelled to testify forty days before or after a session is because that's how long it took to travel by horseback from London to the most northerly part of Scotland. In Canada, the privilege is a holdover from a time when MPs and senators had to travel weeks by train to get to Ottawa. Gordon Barnhard, a former clerk of the Senate and the Saskatchewan Legislature, called the immunity privilege "an anachronism that's outlived its usefulness."

Eric Berntson's only comment about the attempts to serve him with a subpoena was to a reporter with *The Hill Times* weekly newspaper outside the Senate Chamber. "I have nothing to say, not now, not ever. I have no comment. That's it. The long and the short of it. I have no comment. Period."

All the fuss about Clyne Harradence's letter to the court didn't dampen Michael Hopfner's determination to get Berntson into the witness box. He said he was considering asking the judge to issue a warrant for Berntson's arrest. If the judge went along, the RCMP could ask the speaker of the House of Commons for permission to go to Parliament Hill and arrest Berntson, or officers could wait until the senator left the protection of the Hill and then arrest him.

"I believe that Mr. Berntson should come and there is no reason why he shouldn't come . . . ," Hopfner told reporters. Others agreed with him. A Reform MP criticized Berntson in the House of Commons for not agreeing to testify at Hopfner's trial. A New Democratic MP joined in the criticism. Berntson was accused of abusing his privilege by refusing to testify, and there were calls for his resignation.

Before the judge at Michael Hopfner's trial had to decide on whether to issue an arrest warrant, the RCMP found Senator Berntson and served him with the subpoena. His lawyer, Clyne Harradence, then sent a fax to Michael Hopfner stating that Berntson would be available to testify, but that it would take him a few days to arrange to get to Regina. In the meantime, Eric Berntson decided it was time he told his side of the story about the subpoena war. He wrote an open letter to the people of Saskatchewan. It was published in the daily newspapers in Regina and Saskatoon on October 11, 1996.

In light of the events of the past two weeks, I thought it important, as one who has served the people of Saskatchewan for many years, to write to you in an attempt to set the record straight. I chose this route so that I could address you directly, as I always tried to do when I served as a member from Souris-Cannington, in the Saskatchewan Legislature for 16 years.

There are a number of matters that have to be stated:

I have been subpoenaed to appear as a witness at previous trials in Saskatchewan on three occasions, on each occasion I have made arrangement to attend the court at a mutually convenient time. In only one of these instances was I actually required to testify. In these cases, I arranged with the RCMP so that they could effect service of the subpoena at a mutually convenient time and place for service.

I appeared at the court, when required, and as I have indicated, in only one case, was I actually called to give evidence.

In relation to recent events, the Hopfner trial, at no time was there any attempt made to serve me, outside the precincts of Parliament, at home or anywhere else that I am aware of, prior to October 10, 1996. I have carried on my normal routine and, in no way, have I attempted to evade service of a subpoena.

Therefore, the period from September 9, 1996 when the subpoena was issued until October 9, 1996, I had not been served.

I never invoked the privileges as a member of the Senate, not to be compelled to testify when parliament was sitting. First, the privilege would not have applied, because I had not been served with the subpoena. Secondly, it has always been my intent to co-operate as fully as necessary with any court matter. I believe I demonstrated that fact when I appeared and testified at earlier trials in Saskatchewan.

The letter dated September 27, 1996, from Mr. Clyne Harradence, Q.C., acting on my behalf which set out the privileges of a member of Parliament, was written to inform Mr. Hopfner that these privileges do exist and in response to *a threat made to my wife by an unknown person who claimed to be helping Mr. Hopfner, stating that an arrest warrant would be sought if I did not obey the subpoena; a subpoena which had not been served.*

The letter was sent to the court by Mr. Harradence simply to inform the court of the situation and for information only as my position was that of a potential witness, with no status as a party in the trial, who had been threatened with possible arrest.

Mr. Harradence has acted for other witnesses subpoenaed by Mr. Hopfner and has arranged for them to be provided with information by Mr. Hopfner on matters where he was attempting to adduce evidence so that such witnesses could check their records and answer accurately. Mr. Harradence has also arranged a time agreeable to the court for these witnesses to appear and testify. I had not been served with a subpoena as of the letter of September 27, 1996, and it was anticipated that Mr. Hopfner would respond to Mr. Harradence's letter.

Late last evening, the RCMP served the subpoena on me at my residence in Ottawa. The residence which address is no secret and a telephone number which has never been unlisted and where, contrary to certain press allegations, I spend every night when I was in Ottawa.

I can truthfully say that no one enjoyed serving the people of Saskatchewan more than I did during my time in the Saskatchewan Legislature. It was an exciting time of growth and development.

I felt it necessary to write this letter, because of the respect I have for the people of Saskatchewan and so that you would hear directly from me, a recounting of the reality of the last few weeks.

While all the intrigue with the senator was unfolding, Michael Hopfner turned to the other witnesses on his list. Some unexpected twists were about to unfold. The first occurred when Michael McCafferty returned to the witness box. He had earlier testified for the Crown and admitted to receiving a cut of the cash received by filling out false claims for Michael Hopfner. Hopfner now said he had a list of questions he wanted to put to McCafferty.

Hopfner was cautioned several times by Justice Wimmer when Michael McCafferty was in the stand. "I'm sorry. You can't do that," the judge said at one point, interrupting Hopfner, who was making a statement rather than asking a question. Justice Wimmer then told Hopfner he could get in the witness box at any time and tell his side of the story. "I'm frustrated, my lord," Hopfner replied.

When the judge questioned Hopfner further about the intent of his questioning of McCafferty, Hopfner replied that he had received ten pages of questions in a fax from former MLA Gerald Muirhead, the man who had been convicted of fraud because of a saddle. When McCafferty, who was sitting in the witness box just to the left of the judge, heard that Michael Hopfner had received a copy of the questions from Muirhead and was about to announce them in court, he started yelling at Hopfner. The judge called a break and McCafferty, wiping tears from his eyes, left the courtroom.

When the trial resumed a short while later, Michael McCafferty told the court that Gerald Muirhead had been his friend for eighteen years and had treated him like a son. He said he discussed his situation with Muirhead in confidence. "I asked his advice as to what questions I may be asked by the Crown or yourself [Hopfner] and he suggested to me, why don't I think of some of the toughest questions I could be asked and fax him those questions." McCafferty said he faxed the questions to Gerald Muirhead the night before Hopfner's trial started. Muirhead passed the fax along to Michael Hopfner two days later. Crown prosecutor Eric Neufeld objected to Hopfner's tactics with the fax and after hearing arguments from both sides, the judge ruled that "the fax as far as I can see from reading it, is of no significance." Hopfner wouldn't release the fax to reporters. He said he was afraid that if he did he might get in trouble with the judge.

When Michael Hopfner called Gerald Muirhead to the witness box, Michael McCafferty's name came up again, but this time, in connection with a different alleged event. Muirhead told a story he said he got from Michael McCafferty about cash being counted in the caucus office. According to Muirhead, McCafferty told him about one time when he, McCafferty, went to the caucus office at night, where he found John Scraba counting $1,000 and $100 bills. Muirhead told the judge:

It was after the investigation started. I'd say about two years ago. And we talked about it off and on because we talk about two or three times a week. He said he was contacted by Chantal Devine to write a speech for her. He was not feeling well but he decided to do it anyhow. So he went to the Legislative Assembly, got his keys out to go into the caucus office but found out it was open. He stepped inside and then went to his own office and realized there was a light there and opened it and that's where he seen people counting money on his desk.

He was nervous, and Mr. Scraba just said to him, "Would you like to help us count this money? We're getting ready for a bank deposit." He said, "You count the hundreds." And he counted the hundreds and said, "There are thirty-six of them." And he put them into a grey bag. He said, "I was so nervous. I seen a bigger pile of $1,000 bills and I seen money in the big drawer that was there [filing cabinet drawer]. The one that was always kept under bars and lock and key. So," he said, "I got my speech material and I left. I was very nervous and glad to get out of there."

Muirhead told the judge that he believed McCafferty said the incident happened in either 1988 or 1989. He admitted he did not know if the story was true.

When Robert Pickering was called to testify, he said Michael McCafferty had told him a similar story. Pickering said when he was with McCafferty in the cafeteria at the Legislature one day, McCafferty told him about seeing John Scraba counting money.

I don't know exactly the date it happened, but Michael had the flu and Mrs. Devine phoned him up and said she had to

*make some speech at a luncheon the next day and he went
to the Legislature, his office, to get some material. Upon his
arrival there he found that the light was on in the caucus
office and he opened the door. It was not locked. When he
got inside, he noticed some people counting money in one of
the offices. He said they were counting piles of $1,000 bills
and $100 bills and the $1,000 pile was bigger than the hundreds. I asked him who was there. He mentioned John
Scraba but somebody interrupted us and he did not tell me
who the other names were. I was in the cafeteria having
lunch. Michael was there having lunch and I sat with him.
It happened the previous day and it was on his mind so he
told me about it. Somewhere in the '89, '90, '91 range. We
never talked about it again.*

Justice Wimmer initially refused to allow the hearsay evidence but changed his mind after Hopfner argued it pertained to
Michael McCafferty's credibility as a witness. Michael
McCafferty denied ever telling a story about John Scraba and
others counting $1,000 bills in the caucus office one night.

When he was in the witness box, Michael McCafferty had a
story of his own, one that he stood behind as gospel truth but
that others denied. It was about Roy Romanow and a so-called
dirty tricks squad. According to McCafferty, the operation was
dubbed "Operation R-Squared." He said the dirty tricks team
was formed in the late 1980s to smear Roy Romanow, who was
leader of the official opposition, the New Democratic Party.
McCafferty said the team spread false information through
newspaper advertisements and letters to the editor and even
considered hiring a private detective to try to dig up dirt on
Romanow. He said there was talk about trying to find
Romanow's medical records to see if there was anything there
that could be used against him.

McCafferty gave an example of one of the stunts the team
was alleged to have pulled off. He said they ran a letter as an
advertisement in the Saskatoon *StarPhoenix* condemning
Romanow for foreclosing on a farmer when he worked as a
lawyer in Saskatoon. McCafferty said he wrote the ad and one

of the other team members paid for it with money taken from the caucus account. He wouldn't say who directed him to write the letter, other than to say he was a "farmer." A former chief of staff in Romanow's office recalled an incident involving an ad, the letter, the *StarPhoenix*, and a farmer. He said: "[The Tories] kept raising the issue and we [the NDP] could never confirm the accuracy of the information because we could never track down the individual and they would never produce the individual or records to show it ever happened."

Michael McCafferty said the purpose of the letter was to rile farmers and to embarrass Roy Romanow on an agricultural issue. He recalled that the committee was in operation for at least a couple of years. He provided working papers on some of the projects that were being considered. They included preparing ghost articles on Romanow and issues for commentary in major newspapers and periodicals, writing letters to the editor for supporters to submit, and orchestrating a direct mail-out to up to two thousand farmers regarding Romanow and farm foreclosures. Other Tories said the dirty tricks team was nothing but a tall tale spun by a highly imaginative former speechwriter.

Ron Barber, the former president of the Saskatchewan PC Party, was also called to testify. Barber was president of the party for about three and a half years during the 1980s. He told the court that he had concerns about some polling that was done by a company called D-Mail. During questioning by Hopfner, Barber said D-Mail was hired to do telephone polling in about fifteen constituencies. "I wasn't satisfied that the work was getting done," he told Justice Wimmer. "I found out where D-Mail was located, in a house here in Regina. I went over to the house at least twice a day and at no time did I see any phoning done. Yet we got a bill for $40,000." Barber said the PC Party was paying for twenty-one telephone operators. He testified that they might have done the work at night, but he said he never saw the results of the poll. He said it was just after the 1986 election and the party was broke. Barber was reluctant to pay the bill, but Don Pringle, the executive director with the PC Party, hounded him about paying the money. When he asked Don Pringle questions about expenditures, he was told to bug off. Barber said he finally relented and signed the cheque.

Michael Hopfner was having a field day. Justice Wimmer was giving him lots of leeway to call witnesses and to question them, even though a lot of his questions and the answers he received had nothing to do with the case before the court. And when the witnesses were sworn in, Crown prosecutor Eric Neufeld also had a chance to pop some questions. A key part of Hopfner's defence, as he saw it, was to show that there were a lot of things going on in the caucus office that he didn't know about, so therefore how could he be one of the leaders in the fraud scheme? He acknowledged that some of the testimony he wanted to get before the court had nothing to do with the charges against him, but he wanted to use this testimony to show that decisions were being made at a higher level than his own. The judge could sift through the evidence for relevant testimony and the extra information was not hurting the Crown's case. Indeed, many people found these stories from the dark side of politics extremely interesting.

When Hopfner got around to asking questions about the so-called Martensville bank account, more laundry was aired. Ralph Katzman, the man who had handled the money, was called to the witness box. On December 6, 1985, $450,000 was transferred from the PC caucus account in Regina to a bank in Martensville. It was the same bank where Katzman did his personal banking. Katzman told the court that he gave $45,000 of that money to Lorne McLaren, the same Lorne McLaren who had pleaded guilty to fraud and theft and had been sentenced to three and a half years in prison. Katzman said he also gave money to other MLAs, and he said he gave $250,000 to the Saskatchewan Conservative Party to pay for polling. Bank records seized by the RCMP showed there were also withdrawals from the account of $55,000 and $33,000. Katzman said he couldn't recall where that money went and that he had lost the scrap of paper he used to keep track of the transactions. When Michael Hopfner asked him why he didn't tell his former colleagues where the money was located and how it was being spent, Katzman claimed he was investing the money on behalf of the caucus and said: "Those who didn't need to know didn't need to know."

When reporters asked Lorne McLaren about the $45,000 he received from Ralph Katzman, he replied that he got the money after he asked Grant Devine for some help. He said when he was dropped from the cabinet in late 1985, his salary was considerably reduced. "I asked Premier Devine if I could have some compensation because of the downsizing of my salary. If he could help me, if I could have a loan. If I didn't run again, they were going to see if I could fit in somewhere, get a job and so on. I can't even remember if I asked for a certain amount. Then I got a cheque from Mr. Katzman, a personal cheque." McLaren said he didn't know where the money came from until it came up in court at Michael Hopfner's trial. "I talked with Premier Devine," he said. "I didn't talk with Mr. Katzman. When I got the cheque, I thought it was from the PC Party of Saskatchewan." McLaren said he was supposed to send monthly payments to Ralph Katzman, but he couldn't afford to do so at the time. He said he intended to pay the money back.

When Ralph Katzman closed the Martensville account in December 1986, he transferred the remaining $69,139 into his personal bank account. "It's sitting in my bank account waiting for instruction on what to do with it," Katzman told the judge. "The former leader of the party [Rick Swenson] has been told that. I don't know what to do with it. It's just sitting there." He said he asked Swenson twice what to do with the $69,000.

The next day, Rick Swenson showed up at the courthouse to talk with reporters so he could, in his words, "set the record straight." "When I woke up this morning and heard that my name was being thrown around in the courtroom in some way that I didn't feel was appropriate, I was upset," he told reporters. Swenson said Ralph Katzman first told him about the Martensville account in a parking lot in Saskatoon. "I was in Saskatoon—I believe it was in 1994 at an executive meeting—and I met Mr. Katzman there at the Parktown Hotel. After the meeting was over, we had a conversation out in the parking lot, at which time he informed me about a sum of money which he had in his possession." Swenson asked him if it had anything to do with the Communication Allowances and Katzman told him that it did not. It was grant money from that particular caucus period and he had been in charge of it on behalf of caucus.

Swenson said he asked Katzman if the police were aware of the money and he said that they were. "He had been questioned on it and they [the police] had solicited information from him. I asked him if he had gone to a solicitor about it and he said he had. And he wondered what to do with the money. I said, I certainly in my position wasn't prepared to offer him any advice at all on behalf of the current caucus, the 1991 to 1995 caucus that I was leading at the time. Because the police were aware of it and obviously had interviewed him about it, [I told him] that his best route as far as I could see was just to leave it alone. That if they [the police] wished to do something about it, they eventually would get around to it. And if they weren't concerned about it, they wouldn't."

Swenson said he didn't ask Katzman how he got the money. When asked why not, he replied, "Well, Ralph was elected prior to myself by a long time. I only came into the government in a by-election in 1985. Most of [the] period of time he was talking about was prior to me even being an elected member. . . . I guess [the money] had been there for nine years before he told me about it, and if he'd taken responsibility upon himself to manage it and to take it into his own account after nine years I certainly wasn't going to take any responsibility for it or really want anything to do with it. I just didn't think it was appropriate."

Rick Swenson says the second time Ralph Katzman talked with him about the money was at the national policy convention about a month before he testified at Michael Hopfner's trial. He said Katzman told him he still had the $69,000. "I said, well, that's basically your problem, Ralph. I'm no longer an MLA or in any position to advise you on anything. I just assumed that the status of the thing was still the same and the day that he took it into his possession, it became his problem."

"Why didn't you discuss it with your colleagues in the Conservative caucus?" he was asked.

"Because none of them would have been aware of it to begin with and it, to me, wasn't money that belonged to the current caucus in any shape or form."

"Was it because you didn't want anything to do with it?"

"No, not at all," Swenson replied. "I felt that it was being dealt with in a right and proper manner, that the authorities were involved in it, and that he felt some need to share this with me because I was the leader at the time. Mr. Katzman has been a long-time friend of mine and he was obviously feeling bad about the situation and I sympathized with him. Yeah, it was a very uncomfortable situation."

The Saskatchewan Tory Party was quick to distance itself from the Martensville account. The then-leader of the party, Bill Boyd, dashed off a letter to the speaker of the Legislative Assembly. "It has recently come to our attention that Mr. Ralph Katzman is in possession of $69,139 that was received in the form of caucus grants during the period 1982 to 1986." In the letter, Boyd said his caucus had no claim on the money and that it should be returned to the provincial treasury. "On behalf of the PC caucus, I am writing to recommend that you contact Mr. Katzman and request that he return this money to the Legislative Assembly Office."

Ralph Katzman's lawyer sent the $69,139 to the speaker of the Legislative Assembly. As for the $250,000 that Ralph Katzman claimed he had given to the PC Party to pay for polling, Bill Boyd was not as willing to pay that bill. He said the party was fully prepared to return any public money it had received illegally, but he added that it was up to the courts to make that determination. He said they were trying to determine whether the money received from the Martensville account went toward legitimate research expenditures, like non-partisan polling. But he said they were having trouble finding any information because of "shoddy" business practices at the party headquarters during the time in question. "From what I saw, there was more accountability in a children's popcorn stand than there was over there," he said.

Michael Hopfner wasn't finished with the Martensville account yet. When former MLA and caucus chair Myles Morin sat in the witness box, the Martensville account was back in the spotlight. Myles Morin was PC caucus chair when the $450,000 was drawn from the account and given to Ralph Katzman. He said when Katzman came to him and asked for the surplus money, he checked with the premier before he handed it over. Morin said he hadn't known how much caucus money was given to Katzman until the police told him. He said the caucus administrator, Joan Woulds, handled the details of the transaction.

Grant Devine read a front-page story in *The Globe and Mail* about Myles Morin's testimony under the headline "Devine Knew, Witness Says." The next day, October 25, he issued a strongly worded written statement in which he stated unequivocally: "I have never been involved in, approved or condoned, or been aware of any illegal activity in the Legislative Assembly of Saskatchewan."

Grant Devine also denied having anything to do with the $45,000 loan for Lorne McLaren. During his testimony in court, Devine told the judge that McLaren once told him he was having money problems and asked if there was any way he could help. He said he told McLaren that he "didn't know what was possible to help him" and that he couldn't "promise" anything. He said the former caucus chair's financial trouble came up in discussions with caucus members and staff, and that he encouraged them to offer assistance if they could. "I could have, in conversation, said Lorne needs financial help and if there is anything we can do to put him to work, keep it in mind," he said. Afterwards, talking with reporters outside the courthouse, Devine said, "Anything that was done from my recollection was absolutely correct and fine and if it wasn't, that was somebody else's poor judgement."

"Do you accept any responsibility for what went on in the caucus office?" a reporter asked.

"A leader always does," Devine replied. "You feel very responsible and you feel very badly for any mistakes that were made. You can't escape that. There [are] a lot of good people who do a lot of good work. As you know, from time to time mistakes are made and the responsibility eventually comes to me, and I understand that. But the good work and the sincere efforts for a whole lot of people for years and years shouldn't be overlooked, and I won't overlook that."

"Is this what you're going to be remembered for?"

"There are risks going into public life," Devine replied. "And you bear it. You wear it. So I've had some ups and downs. And this is not a lot of fun, but you can't be intimidated by this." Devine did say he felt a "little betrayed and hurt."

Outside the courthouse, Myles Morin refused to comment on anything he said while in the witness box. "When you left after being defeated in 1986, did you get any money or loans?" a reporter asked Morin. "No, I didn't. Not one dime. Never got any cash. Never did anything wrong. Had no knowledge of anything that was going on here." And with that, he left. Morin, like most of the Tories who testified at Hopfner's trial, did not want to be tied to the fraud scandal. He certainly didn't want to be seen talking about it on the six o'clock news.

When it was Senator Eric Berntson's turn to walk up the courthouse steps and sit in the witness box, reporters and television cameras chased him from his vehicle to the courthouse doors, a distance of about a half a block. They fired a barrage of questions at him. "I think you'll hear all the answers in the courthouse" was his only comment.

When Berntson sat in the witness box, he didn't say much. He just repeated most of what he had said when he testified at John Scraba's preliminary hearing. His testimony was quite a letdown after all the ruckus created by Michael Hopfner in his efforts to get Berntson to testify. When he finished questioning the senator, Michael Hopfner admitted there was nothing special about having Berntson appear, except maybe just getting him there. Hopfner acknowledged that he had wanted Berntson to testify, adding that the more Berntson fought having to testify, the more Hopfner wanted to force him to do it. In the end, he described the senator's testimony as "uneventful." He said without the media pressure, Berntson would not have testified, and he thanked the media for, as he said, "bringing Mr. Berntson to me."

When Senator Berntson left the courthouse, he was hounded once again by reporters with microphones and cameras all the way to his vehicle. Mostly he ignored them. When he did respond to their questions, his remarks were rapier sharp. As he opened the door to his vehicle, he gave a parting thrust, "I've been properly treated by everybody but the media."

Then he got into his vehicle, closed the door, and drove away.

After all the former colleagues he wanted to call had testified, it was Michael Hopfner's turn. He couldn't ask himself questions, so he worked it out with the judge that the young woman who had chased Berntson would play the lawyer for a while. Sitting in the witness box, the tired former PC caucus whip tried to explain the $1,000 bills he had deposited into his personal bank account and to respond to police allegations that it was money he had received from John Scraba. Hopfner said if he had the caucus books he was sure he could clear himself, but the books had been destroyed just before the Tories were defeated in 1991. At one point during the trial, Hopfner told reporters that if he had received money illegally, he wouldn't have taken it in $1,000 bills. "Even [in] the gangster movies, for God's sake," he said, "they don't want $1,000 bills. They want it in all these smaller denominations that can't be traced."

Michael Hopfner, like the other Tories who had sat in the witness box before him, put some of the blame for what happened on an MLA's workload. "Unless you've been one," he said, "you can't understand." And with that heavy workload, he said, he didn't have the time to check on every detail of what was done in the caucus office. Hopfner, like the others, said he trusted John Scraba and Joan Woulds to ensure things were done properly.

When Hopfner's accountant, the one who was helping him build his case, testified, he described his friend as "a man without any business savvy." The accountant did the books for Hopfner's hotel in Lashburn. His friend said, "I believe he is innocent. I believe he is totally innocent. Anyone who has followed this case can see the level of Mr. Hopfner's business knowledge. It just doesn't fit."

But the accountant's arguments and Michael Hopfner's long list of witnesses didn't sway Justice Wimmer. On November 15, 1996, Michael Hopfner was found guilty of illegally receiving $57,348 from caucus employees after submitting false expense claims. He was cleared on the other fraud charge and on the charge of conspiracy to commit fraud. The judge advised Hopfner to muster all his resources and get some legal advice before he came back for sentencing or the consequences could be dire.

Standing in the courtroom, behind the podium he used to mount his own defence and staring at the judge, Michael Hopfner was on the verge of tears. Later, talking with reporters, Hopfner defended his decision not to hire a lawyer. He said if he had hired a lawyer, all the "filth" wouldn't have been revealed. He thanked Justice Wimmer for giving him the leeway to allow the "crap" to surface.

In December 1996, in between Michael Hopfner's verdict and his sentencing hearing, Ray Meiklejohn lost his appeal before the Saskatchewan Court of Appeal. "I'm just very disappointed," he said, after a panel of three judges dismissed his appeal. "It's not the outcome that I would have liked, certainly. And it's not the outcome that I feel we should have had. However, so be it." When asked if he would ever consider getting involved in politics again, he replied that "the furthest thing from my mind would be ever becoming involved again. I have no interest in it."

Early in the new year, on January 6, 1997, Michael Hopfner arrived at the courthouse for sentencing. This time he had a lawyer with him. Al McIntyre argued for a conditional sentence with electronic monitoring. Crown prosecutor Eric Neufeld argued that Hopfner should be sent to jail for more than eighteen months and that he should be ordered to pay back $56,000.

Before he announced Hopfner's sentence, Justice Wimmer made a few comments. "Politics," he said, "should be regarded as a worthy pursuit engaged in only by honourable men and women, inspired by the opportunity for public service. Regrettably," he continued, "episodes of the sort we heard about in this case can only foster cynicism and distrust and perhaps discourage the best among us from seeking public office."

The judge added that if it were in his power, he would strip Michael Hopfner of his MLA pension. He said he was certain that many people would find it hard to understand "that a person elected and entrusted with public office can pillage the public purse and then at the end of it all retire with a pension financed in part from public funds." He went on to say, "Constituents want to trust their elected representatives." He added, "The public is entitled to expect that any corruptions of these trusts will be soundly denounced." He sentenced Michael Hopfner to eighteen months in a provincial correctional centre and ordered him to pay $56,000 restitution to the Government of Saskatchewan.

Continuing to look straight at Michael Hopfner, who stared back in apparent disbelief at what he was hearing, the judge said, "Today will be counted among the worst days of your life. But you will put it behind you. Time does heal and people do forgive and forget. You still have many good days and good years ahead of you." Michael Hopfner was taken away in handcuffs.

At the side door of the courthouse, as Hopfner was being directed into a van by a police officer, a reporter asked him what he felt about the decision. "Well, Mr. Wimmer [the judge] has made his decision. I don't agree with what happened with the decision. But I guess you got to either have maybe a lot of money to afford lawyers or know how to defend yourself. I'll be deciding about the future here and an appeal. . . . I have more information that I didn't have at the time and I found out after and whether that will hold any ice for an appeal or not I don't know yet. I'll talk to a lawyer about that and see where we go from there."

"The judge had some harsh words about you," another reporter shouted. "He said if he could he would take your pension, you breached the public trust. What are your thoughts on that?"

"Well, I guess I just did not give him and convince him enough I did not do what he believes I did do and I don't hold anything against him for that."

"You still maintain, despite everything the judge said and all the evidence and everything else, you did nothing wrong. You are an innocent man going to prison?"

"That's right. I tell you, if they hang a guy for this, they'd be hanging an innocent man. And that's [it] as far as I'm concerned."

The judge's comment about Michael Hopfner's MLA pension received a mixed reaction on the streets and in the coffeehouses. Hopfner was entitled to a pension of between $800 and $900 a month. It kicked in when he turned fifty in January 1997. Premier Roy Romanow came to Hopfner's defence on the pension issue. "My view is that the pension contributions of MLAs are like the pension contributions of other employees, or people who are members of pension plans," Romanow said. "They are earned. They are contributed to. They are part of the terms of employment. They are deferred income for the time that a person retires. And they are separate and apart from criminal proceedings." The premier added, "There is no indication that the pension for Mr. Hopfner was acquired in any other way but under the normal rules of the Legislative Assembly, properly, correctly, legally, and lawfully. And to strip an MLA of pension over and above any sanctions that he or she may receive under criminal law, I think is a hardship which is imposed upon, not only on the MLA, but perhaps on an innocent family."

Michael Hopfner was the sixth person convicted of fraud as the result of Project Fiddle. As he was settling into his jail cell, another former colleague was getting ready to face the judge.

John Gerich Tries a Jury

As the trials proceeded, former PC caucus whip John Gerich listened to the news reports on radio and television and read the newspaper stories as one after another of his former colleagues was branded a criminal and was either sent to jail, fined, or both. These were people he had debated political issues with around the cabinet table and celebrated victories with during the Tory years in Saskatchewan. He knew some of their families, what they did for fun, and in some cases, their dreams and aspirations. He had come to admire and respect many of them during their years together in Grant Devine's caucus. Now, in early 1997, it was Gerich's turn to face the judge. But this time, the former RCMP officer was on the other side of the law.

John Gerich, a tall, nearly bald, unassuming middle-aged man, had served as the MLA for Redberry, a farming area, from 1982 until he lost his seat in the 1991 general election. He and his family had built a good life in the small central Saskatchewan community of Blaine Lake.

When Gerich left the Royal Canadian Mounted Police, after five years in the force, he returned to farming and got a job as a full-time manager of a grain elevator. During his years in politics, he served as caucus whip and was appointed associate minister of economic development and tourism. That was in 1989. He also served as a member of a number of committees, including the Order-in-Council Review Committee, the board of directors for the Saskatchewan Property Management Corporation, and the board of directors for the Futures Corporation. According to RCMP documents and later court testimony, during his later years in politics, he was also a willing participant in the fraud scheme that played out in the caucus office. Police said he knew about the pooling system, the numbered companies, and the money-laundering plan. He was facing charges of fraud, conspiring with John Scraba to commit fraud, and illegally obtaining cash, a computer hard drive, and a portable, electronic public address system worth a total of $12,264 by submitting false expense claims through his Communication Allowance.

During interviews with police officers before he was charged, John Gerich admitted that over the years he had contributed a portion of his Communication Allowance to the pool and that he knew about the numbered companies set up in the caucus office. But he said he never looked into what happened to the money after it went to the numbered companies. During a taped interview with a police officer in the early days of Project Fiddle, Gerich told the officer, "What we did is we put a lot of trust in John Scraba, who was handling all this. We had other things to do. . . . It might have not been run in a good business sense. But myself as a whip, I should have maybe been more interested in what was happening in some of these companies." He described himself as a "team player" who went along with the pooling plan in order to get "a better bang for your dollar" to pay for group advertising.

In early 1988, about a year after the pooling system was set up, John Gerich reported to caucus on the status of the pool. He made an oral presentation and handed out a written report, showing expenditures. Gerich said John Scraba had prepared the report. According to police, the report should have raised some eyebrows. It showed that one of the first bills paid was $16,700 to Mercury Graphics for printing *Viewpoint*, the PC Party newspaper, a clear violation of the rule prohibiting Communication Allowance money from being spent on partisan advertising. The report also showed that $17,000 of the Communication Allowance money collected for the pool in 1987 had been carried over into 1988. Under the rules of the Legislature, MLAs could only get money out of their Communication Allowance to pay for work that had already been done. When he testified at John Scraba's preliminary hearing, Gerich was the only MLA to acknowledge that the pooling system required the use of false invoices in order to accumulate a surplus.

As his court date drew near, John Gerich spent a lot of time discussing his situation with Judy Gerich, his wife of twenty-eight years. Money was tight in the Gerich household as John had had trouble finding work after he was defeated in the 1991 provincial election. He had managed to find a few part-time jobs, but they didn't pay much. Judy was a school principal and a teacher at a Hutterite colony north of Saskatoon and was the family's main breadwinner. After much discussion, the couple decided they couldn't afford to hire a lawyer, and Judy took a leave of absence from her job to handle her husband's defence. John Gerich also decided to put his case before a jury, the first Tory charged in Project Fiddle to do so. The trial began on January 20, 1997.

Crown prosecutor Sharon Pratchler handled this one. The short, soft-spoken woman, who had assisted Eric Neufeld in some of the previous Tory fraud cases, took over as the prosecutor for Project Fiddle when Neufeld, a senior prosecutor in the justice department, moved on to other cases. At the start of the trial, Pratchler told reporters not to expect any surprises. She said the case was in the documents and she was going to handle it just like any other case. She said, "[I'm going to] put my head down and put the evidence in."

In her opening statement to the jury, Pratchler stated that the case was all about false invoices and how they were used to obtain public money. She urged the nine women and three men on the jury to follow the money. As he had done in all the previous cases, Sergeant John Leitch laid out the Crown's case using an overhead projector and television monitors strategically positioned around the courtroom. Leitch traced the flow of money from Gerich's alleged false claims from the Legislature into the numbered companies in the caucus office, and then into the PC caucus bank account, and finally into bank accounts belonging to John and Judy Gerich. The banking records for the Geriches that were seized by the RCMP showed that a few days after one of Gerich's Communication Allowance claims was paid through a numbered company, he would deposit a similar amount in his personal bank account.

On January 23, 1997, while the Crown was introducing its

case against John Gerich, the RCMP announced that six more Tories had been charged. Beattie Martin, who had served as a cabinet minister in the Devine government, and Michael McCafferty were charged with fraud over $5,000. The police wouldn't release the names of the other four because their summonses had not been served. The next day two more names were released. Robert Andrew, who also served as a cabinet minister, was charged with fraud under $5,000. Don Pringle, who served as a special advisor to Grant Devine, was charged with fraud over $5,000 and breach of trust. Within days, reporters learned the other two accused were Senator Eric Berntson and former cabinet minister Bob Pickering. These latest charges brought the total number of people accused in Project Fiddle to nineteen: sixteen former MLAs and three caucus employees.

The calls for Berntson to step aside as deputy Conservative leader in the Senate started immediately. One of the first of them came from Reform MP Elwin Hermanson. Provincial Conservative Leader Bill Boyd agreed. Federal Conservative Leader Jean Charest responded quickly. He announced that Berntson would continue to serve as a senator while the charges worked their way through the court, but confirmed that Berntson had resigned as deputy opposition leader.

Back in Saskatchewan, when John Scraba was called to testify at John Gerich's trial, he told the jurors that he gave Gerich cash that he had obtained through false Communication Allowance claims. He also told them that Gerich was one of several MLAs present during a discussion in the caucus office in early 1987 about setting up the numbered companies for the PC caucus.

Pratchler argued that Gerich knew the rules for MLA allowances because, from 1986 to 1989, he was a member of the Board of Internal Economy. He also served as caucus whip for that same period with signing authority on the caucus account. Pratchler accused Gerich of signing cheques for cash on the caucus account, adding that some of the money ended up in the pockets of MLAs, including Gerich's own. According to the RCMP's interpretation of the documents they seized, Gerich deposited six $1,000 bills in his personal bank account between

1987 and 1991. The police believed that the bills, which were in sequence with the $1,000 bills the police found in the two safety deposit boxes, came from false expense claims made by John Scraba.

When it was Judy Gerich's turn to present the defence's case, she admitted she was nervous. Even though Court of Queen's Bench Justice William Matheson allowed her lots of lee-way in the courtroom, she said it was a frustrating process for her and her husband. "Well, it's quite unsettling and a person has to deal with it. Day-by-day we deal with it, try to score a few points and clarify a few situations that have arisen over the last week and a half." When a reporter asked John Gerich whether he was going to testify in his own defence, he replied, "We have no idea. We are kinda planning this out as we go and see how our strategy works out."

In their defence before the jury, the Geriches relied heavily on character witnesses. They tried to prove that John was not the kind of person who would get involved in anything shady. They called as witnesses former RCMP officers John had worked with when he was in the force and people he had worked with while he was in politics and since he left politics. Judy Gerich said she wanted to "tell the people [in the jury] what he was like as a person before, during, and after politics." She said the wit-nesses were "people from all walks of life. They're not our friends, so to speak, that we pulled out of the closet."

Judy Gerich also wanted to look for cracks in the Crown's case, especially the paper trail for the $1,000 bills that the Crown alleged her husband had received illegally. But when she announced her plan to sit in the witness box to tell her story about the money, the judge turned her down. He told her she couldn't be a witness and defence lawyer at the same time. If she wanted to testify, she had to stop acting as her hus-band's lawyer.

In the end, a disappointed Judy Gerich decided not to testify. "What I wanted to deal with were personal deposits. John and I both know where they came from and they had nothing to do with caucus funds," she told reporters later outside the court-house. She said one deposit involved cash her husband received when their son sold a car and gave his dad money to repay a loan. And another two she explained as money her husband received for his duties when the Legislature was in session and for per diems for MLA expenses. "And that's what I was going to present." When asked how she felt about the judge's decision that she couldn't be a witness and handle her husband's defence at the same time, she replied, "It cuts you back and you begin to wonder about the truth behind justice. Do we hear the whole story or do we hear part of it?"

When all the evidence was before the jury, Judy Gerich told reporters she was glad the trial was coming to an end. "It's probably the biggest relief and weight off my shoulders that I've had in a long time," she said. "It's been a tough two and a half weeks because I don't think on my feet legally, the way the court runs, and so I've had the rug pulled out from under my feet several times. And we've done a bit of scrambling, but we've given it our best shot." She also took a shot at the use of computer spreadsheets in the courtroom. "You can make a computer walk, talk and sing and lie if you will."

During her final arguments before the jury, Judy Gerich described her husband as a "people person" who was perhaps "naïve about the real world of politics." Drawing a circle on a flip chart in classroom style and writing names inside and outside the circle, she tried to convince the jury that her husband wasn't part of the inner circle in the caucus office that set up the fraud scheme and made it work. "If he is guilty of anything," she said, "it's trusting people like John Scraba and Lorne McLaren."

Later, outside the courthouse, reporters wanted to know why the Geriches hadn't hired a lawyer and whether they had any regrets about their decision. "Well, lawyers cost a lot of money," John Gerich replied. "I'll be up front with you. We've been struggling all our life as a farming couple. To hire a lawyer with great lawyer ability and criminal activity would cost you anywhere from $50,000 to $100,000. We haven't got that kind of cash. So we presented our case the best we can. If we suffer for it, well, we didn't suffer by losing $100,000. And if we are acquitted, then we didn't have to spend $100,000 that we never had."

February 5, 1997, was the day the members of the jury began their deliberations. In his direction to the jury, Justice Matheson said it was "more than coincidence" that certain communications claims made by Gerich ended up in his bank account as cash deposits instead of being used to pay advertising bills. He also pointed out that several witnesses testified that Gerich attended a meeting with several others, including Michael Hopfner and Lorne McLaren, to discuss setting up numbered companies where money gathered through false claims could be pooled. He instructed the jury to ignore the evidence given by character witnesses and to deal with the facts.

It took the jury seven hours to find John Gerich guilty on two of the three charges against him. In the second day of their deliberations, they concluded that Gerich was one of the key players who engineered the fraud scheme to defraud the taxpayers of over $837,000. They also found him guilty of receiving a personal gain of about $12,000 in cash and equipment using false expense claims. They cleared him on the charge of conspiring with John Scraba to defraud taxpayers.

"I'm in shock. What can I say?" John Gerich told reporters after the verdict was announced. "It's a travesty if you look back on my history and my work ethic. You join the Mounted Police and you do a good job. You join the government as a politician and work really hard. Any job I've held I tried to do it to the best of my ability. And then I was duped by Scraba."

Judy Gerich, standing by her husband's side, her face expressionless, said she was not surprised by the verdicts because she thought the judge told the jury in his charge that her husband was guilty of fraud but not conspiracy to commit fraud. "So, I wasn't surprised that it came as that," she said. "I'm just a little bit disappointed in the justice system that if you're an ordinary person, you really don't get to tell your story." She was referring to not being allowed to give evidence from the witness box about the $1,000 deposits in their personal bank accounts.

"We couldn't show our side of it," John Gerich told reporters. "That's maybe a mistake in strategy you do as amateurs." As the scrum with the reporters concluded, Gerich took a shot at politics. "I was told one time when you run for politics it's like walking down the street naked and everybody is throwing rocks at you and when you're done, they're still throwing rocks at you."

When John Gerich came back to court for his sentencing hearing on February 21, he had a lawyer, Hugh Gabruch, at his side. "The evidence proved to the jury beyond a shadow of a doubt that I was guilty in part of this," Gerich told the waiting reporters. "Well, then, I've got to take my lumps. I was in a responsible position. I guess that's life. If the judge says [so], maybe I was reckless in my duties. And from what I see now in hindsight, I probably was reckless." Fighting back tears, Judy Gerich told the reporters that the case had been very difficult on a personal level, but she said, "You can't break the spirit that's between two people. So we will survive this and move on. I'll miss him of course." She knew that her husband was going to jail.

Inside the courtroom, the judge had harsh words for John Gerich. He said the fraud scandal in the Saskatchewan government had stained Canada's political reputation. "Political corruption is endemic to Latin American countries, Asian jurisdictions, and perhaps Eastern European jurisdictions," he remarked, "but never has it been seriously suggested that corruption permeates Canadian politics—at least until a fraud of this scale was revealed." He told John Gerich that his actions contributed to the erosion of public confidence in the political system. Because he betrayed the trust of the people who elected him, he should spend some time in custody. He also said that while Gerich was one of the players in the fraud scheme, he wasn't totally responsible for it.

While his wife and his two adult sons sat in the courtroom, John Gerich read a prepared statement: "I would like to apologize to this court, to my family, my friends, my neighbours and the people of Saskatchewan for the anguish and disappointment that I have caused through these trial proceedings and the things that have happened over the last eleven years."

John Gerich was sentenced to two years less a day in a provincial correctional centre. The Crown prosecutor had asked the judge to order Gerich to pay restitution of nearly $600,000, the difference between the total fraud committed and the money found in the two bank safety deposit boxes. But the judge replied that there was no point imposing a large restitution order because Gerich had earned just $10,000 in each of the last two years and had no future job prospects. He ordered Gerich to pay back the $12,264 he received using phony expense claims. About an hour later, John Gerich, wearing a long winter parka with the hood hanging down over his back and in handcuffs, was escorted by police officers out the back door of the courthouse and into a waiting police van.

Sherwin Petersen's
Forensic Team

Sherwin Petersen, another former Tory cabinet minister netted in Project Fiddle, had been watching John Gerich's trial closely. Petersen was next on the Tory court docket on charges similar to those that sent Michael Hopfner and John Gerich to jail. Things did not look good. Petersen, however, was determined to mount a vigorous defence. The tall, heavy-set, forty-four-year-old farmer with a receding hairline put most of his farm up for sale to raise the money to hire not just one, but two lawyers. One was Clyne Harradence, the courtroom veteran from Prince Albert; the other was Kevin Mellor, a Regina lawyer who specialized in accounting. Harradence called the defence team the "forensic investigators." The date for the face-off was set for February 10, 1997.

"No one has had the financial where-with-all to fight them," Harradence told reporters. "My client has put up the family farm, which has been two generations in their name, for sale, because he isn't going to allow it to happen if he can prevent it. We're going to have a go at it," he added with fire in his eyes. "That's the kind of fight I like."

Sherwin Petersen was first elected in the rural constituency of Kelvington-Wadena in the 1982 Conservative sweep and was re-elected in the next provincial election. He was defeated when the New Democrats took over in 1991. While in government, he spent some time as legislative secretary to the minister of agriculture before being appointed highways minister in 1989.

Petersen faced two counts of fraud over $5,000 and one count of conspiracy to commit fraud. On the first fraud charge, he was accused of using false expense claims to get cash, a video camera, a computer, and a computer hard drive through his Communication Allowance. The investigating officers also alleged that he received two $1,000 bills from John Scraba and that the bills were deposited in his personal bank account. The serial numbers on the bills were in sequence with the numbers on the bills found in the two safety deposit boxes. The second fraud charge and the conspiracy charge were related to the $837,000 diverted through John Scraba to the numbered companies.

At the start of Petersen's trial on February 10, 1997, Harradence requested a delay of at least two months so that his forensic team could sift through hundreds of government records. He also informed Court of Queen's Bench Justice Omer Archambault that he had learned that some of the documents the defence wanted to examine had been destroyed by officials at the Finance Department. Three days earlier, Petersen's legal team had subpoenaed the province's assistant provincial auditor and a representative of the Finance Department requesting documents dated between 1981 and 1996. Finance Department documents are routinely destroyed after seven years. Petersen's lawyers wanted documents going back sixteen years. The legal team also wanted documents the provincial auditor was not willing to hand over. In the end, the provincial auditor's office sent a lawyer to court to intervene because the auditor was concerned about releasing certain "working documents" because of confidentiality.

Harradence argued that without all the documents he had requested from the provincial auditor's office and the Department of Finance, he could not mount a proper defence, and he hinted that he might even ask the judge to drop the charges against his client. Harradence also suggested that his team be given access to RCMP computers, which he described as the police officers' notebooks for the twenty-first century. Crown prosecutor Sharon Pratchler suggested they all get together over the next month or so and see what they could work out. The judge promised a decision the next morning on the request for an adjournment.

Talking with reporters outside the courthouse, Harradence

accused the RCMP of brushing aside allegations that the NDP had done the same things as the Tories with their MLA allowances. "There are now so many facets," he warned. "It's becoming almost a position where the Legislature of Saskatchewan should be approached to appoint a commission to have the whole unsavoury mess fully investigated."

The next morning, Justice Archambault granted a three-month adjournment. He directed both sides to come back to court on April 1 to report on their progress. When they returned three months later, however, the problems continued. Harradence had run into roadblocks in his attempts to obtain the minutes of certain private meetings of the Board of Internal Economy, the all-party committee that set the rules for MLA allowances. On top of that, he was having difficulties obtaining records of certain financial transactions from the branch of the Royal Bank where the caucus and the numbered companies had had their accounts.

Access to RCMP documents was also proving to be a sticking point. Harradence accused the Crown of failing to provide full disclosure on documents it knew about and other evidence. On February 12, Kevin Mellor had sent a letter to Sergeant John Leitch requesting all RCMP computers, disks, investigative documents, and investigative notes that contained information on Sherwin Petersen. Sharon Pratchler argued that the RCMP had provided full disclosure to the defence. She described the request for police computers as a "totally impractical approach to disclosure," adding that to comply would shut down police departments across the country. She suggested instead that the judge could make decisions on the relevancy of any missing information during the trial.

Justice Archambault listened to both sides and then set the trial date for May 20. He urged Clyne Harradence, who was arguing for yet another adjournment, to get any pre-trial motions he was planning to make submitted as soon a possible.

Clyne Harradence was in a sparring mood when he faced reporters in a testy exchange outside the courthouse.

"Can you tell us why you want the adjournment?" a television reporter asked.

"You weren't in court?"

"I was but the [television] camera wasn't," the reporter fired back.

"What we're endeavouring to do is to allow the experts we have now been fortunate enough to acquire in assisting us to make a review of areas that we think haven't been covered by the investigative branch [the RCMP], which will provide us with very strong evidence in support of our client's defence."

"Are you sure there is something there, that this is not just a fishing expedition?" another reporter asked.

"Oh, now, come on. You sound like a prosecutor. Of course there is something there." Harradence added that before it was all over he hoped to prove that it wasn't the people of Saskatchewan that were defrauded, it was the caucus of the Devine government.

Clyne Harradence was back in court on May 2, 1997, requesting that the fraud charges against Sherwin Petersen be dropped "on the basis that relevant evidence has been destroyed." The relevant evidence, according to Harradence, was among documents that had been destroyed by the provincial Finance Department. Harradence argued that RCMP investigators, who had a chance to see all the finance documents, were told of the department's policy to destroy documents after seven years but did nothing. "That is either neglect, wilful blindness, or even something worse than that," he argued before the judge. "It may be an actual offence." If Harradence didn't win a stay, he at least wanted Justice Archambault to direct the RCMP to hand over its computers.

A lawyer for the federal justice department argued that if Sherwin Petersen's defence team were granted access to RCMP computers, the impact on all criminal prosecutions would be "staggering." Then Crown prosecutor Sharon Pratchler jumped into the debate to take issue with Harradence's accusations that the RCMP and the Crown had failed to provide full disclosure. She argued against any further delay in getting the trial underway. Justice Archambault replied that he would hand down a decision as soon as possible.

While the judge was pondering Harradence's application,

another of Sherwin Petersen's former colleagues pleaded guilty to fraud. On May 8, 1997, former Conservative justice minister Bob Andrew admitted to signing a false expense claim for $4,224.27.

Fifty-three-year-old Andrew, a tall, thin man who looks like he is always in a hurry, served as the MLA for Kindersley from 1978 to 1989, when he resigned from active politics. He was justice minister from 1986 to 1989. He also served as minister of finance and as minister of economic development. When he departed provincial politics, he was given an appointment as a trade officer for the Saskatchewan government in Minneapolis in the United States. When the New Democrats came to power in 1991, they closed the office and Andrew was let go, but the Tories took care of him. The Brian Mulroney government appointed Andrew a temporary member of the National Energy Board in Calgary in March 1992 and made him a full-time member the following year in a position that was to last until the year 2000.

Bob Andrew admitted he signed a phony expense claim to draw $4,224.27 from his Communication Allowance just before he quit politics in December 1989. He said he took the money to give it to his constituency secretary. When Andrew left the Tory cabinet in 1989, he had to lay her off. He said he wanted to give her a severance package but because she was hired by an order in council, she didn't qualify. On December 1, 1989, Andrew claimed reimbursement of $4,500 for communications and consulting work under his MLA Communication Allowance. The false expense claim was processed through Dome Advertising, a company with close ties to the Conservatives. Andrew submitted a false invoice to the Legislative Assembly and received a cheque for $4,224.27, the amount of money left in his Communication Allowance for 1989. He used the money to pay his secretary three months' salary. Bob Andrew says he handled the whole transaction on his own, without any help from anyone. The police had found the false expense claim in the pile of documents collected for the Project Fiddle investigation. At the time of the offence, Andrew had already stepped down from his cabinet posts, although he was still sitting as an MLA.

In the courtroom, Bob Andrew's lawyer argued for a conditional discharge so that his client wouldn't have a criminal record. Crown prosecutor Sharon Pratchler argued that a conditional discharge would send the wrong message to the public. She posed the question "If those charged with the responsibility to make laws don't obey them, then who will?" It had become a favourite phrase for Pratchler when hauling former MLAs before a judge. In this case it had an extra resonance as Bob Andrew had been minister of justice in Grant Devine's government.

Provincial Court Judge Diane Morris agreed with Sharon Pratchler. On May 23, 1997, she fined Bob Andrew $5,000 and ordered him to pay restitution of $4,224.27. She said that Andrew had held a position of trust and had committed a serious breach of that trust. Adding that he had violated both the principles of honesty and of integrity, she said, "I don't know of a more distasteful duty than to impose sentence on a former justice minister."

Outside the courthouse, Bob Andrew tried to ignore the journalists who were waiting for him as he hurried toward his car. The reporters, some with television cameras, followed firing questions at him. One reporter asked how he felt about some of the judge's comments.

"I've had harsh words said about me before," he said scurrying along the sidewalk. "I got to get on with my life. That's the long and the short of it."

"Do you think it's fair?"

"If you're going to spend your life worrying about whether life is fair to you or not fair to you, you're not going to get very far," he replied. "I shouldn't have done what I did. I did it. I 'fessed up to it. You get your punishment. You take it on the chin and you get on with life."

When he had been charged in January 1997, Andrew had taken a leave from his job with the National Energy Board. In May, he was on holiday leave and receiving full salary. He was fired a week after he entered his guilty plea. When asked what he was going to do, he gave a short laugh, "I'm going to go back to Calgary and look for a job. Got any ideas?" He accused the provincial government of criminalizing the political system in

Saskatchewan, but he refused to comment further, saying he would only get himself into more trouble.

Meanwhile, in the ongoing saga of Sherwin Petersen's trial, Justice Archambault ordered the RCMP to give the defence team any documents about Project Fiddle that hadn't been handed over previously. Harradence, however, did not get access to the computers of the investigating officers, and the judge said he could not rule on the request to drop the charges against Petersen until after he heard evidence at the trial. But the judge did say that he viewed the destruction of documents by the provincial Finance Department as troubling. He questioned why the RCMP didn't have the documents saved or at least why they didn't tell the Finance Department to save them because of the investigation. An official with the Finance Department explained that the police weren't told about the government policy for destroying documents until after some of the documents had already been shredded.

Outside the courthouse, when reporters asked Harradence about the destruction of documents, he accused the police of conducting a very poor investigation. "I don't think the people of Saskatchewan were defrauded of one nickel," he said. "Every nickel that came into that caucus office were legitimate payments on behalf of the people of Saskatchewan to a political party that was running the affairs of this province. But there was a clique that was running that office. The fraud was as much against the MLAs who were charged as against the people of Saskatchewan." Harradence suggested that if journalists wanted an issue, they should be demanding a full inquiry into what happened in the caucus office and the police investigation. Harradence and his team then left the courthouse to prepare Petersen's defence.

Sherwin Petersen's trial finally got underway on May 20, 1997. But it was soon bogged down in more legal wrangling. This time it was over the RCMP's access to and handling of exhibits. The exhibits—stacks of files and documents, some in binders—were in bookcases and boxes in the courtroom. When they were not needed in the courtroom, they were kept in another room in the building. Clyne Harradence told the judge that he was concerned because police officers had free range of the exhibits that were in the court's possession. "I question the validity of those exhibits now," Harradence said. "I'm getting a little tired of allegations of wrongdoing without evidence to support it," Sharon Pratchler fired back. The judge, after checking with the court clerk, said he was satisfied that the exhibits were being handled properly.

The much-delayed trial finally got underway, and RCMP Sergeant John Leitch was the Crown's first witness. He laid out the case, as he had done many times in the past, with boxes of documents, his laptop computer, a slide projector, and television monitors. When it was Clyne Harradence's turn to cross-examine Leitch, he accused Leitch of conducting a "witch hunt against the PC caucus." He wanted to know if the chief investigator for Project Fiddle had conducted a proper investigation or whether he had simply formed an opinion based on his own "tunnel vision." Leitch calmly replied that the "fruits" of his investigation had been given to the Crown, and that after the Crown had reviewed the evidence, he laid charges. But Clyne Harradence had only just begun. During his cross-examination, he tried to link Leitch's alleged pursuit of charges against Conservatives to Jack Wolfe's suicide. "He has done tremendous harm if he's wrong," Harradence said. "One man even killed himself."

Sergeant John Leitch was visibly shaken by Harradence's attack using Jack Wolfe. The police officer asked the judge if he could respond to the accusations. Harradence objected but the judge allowed it. Leitch said that he believed he told Harradence that he didn't think Jack Wolfe had committed an offence. He said he had asked Harradence to ask Jack Wolfe if he would agree to an interview for purposes that were more general. He stressed that Jack Wolfe was never charged with anything.

Harradence's attack on Leitch using Jack Wolfe angered Sharon Pratchler. She demanded that he apologize to Leitch. She noted that Harradence didn't mention the nine people who had been convicted in the police investigation. Harradence fired back that many of the people who were convicted didn't have the resources to defend themselves. Justice Archambault interrupted and told Harradence to move on. Outside the courthouse, Sharon Pratchler was reluctant to discuss details of the case with reporters. "It's in the documents," she told reporters during a lunch break. "It's all about false invoices. That's the allegation of the Crown."

During the trial, Clyne Harradence had some tough questions for a number of the Crown's other witnesses, including Marilyn Borowski. Borowski, the director of Financial Services for the Legislative Assembly, was one of the people who had launched Project Fiddle by talking about her concerns regarding Tory spending with Paul Raphael de Montigny and his wife in the lounge of the Regina Inn in the spring of 1991. When it was his turn to cross-examine Borowski, Harradence accused her of being on a campaign. "You continued your campaign against only one party," he shot at her. "I did not continue a campaign against any party," she replied, adding that she hadn't wanted the conversation in the hotel lounge to be made public and had no idea that would happen. She said she believed the couple was bound by the same oath of secrecy as she was since they were both government employees. She did not know that Paul Raphael de Montigny, an employee with the provincial Crown corporation SaskPower, had not taken an oath of secrecy. Borowski admitted that she should not have discussed her concerns with the couple. She said her boss had talked with her about the incident but she wasn't disciplined.

When it was John Scraba's turn in the witness box, Lorne McLaren and his wife, Barbara, were in the courtroom. Barbara was on holidays from her job as a clerk in a car wash in Fort Qu'Appelle, about a forty-five minute drive north of Regina. Lorne was still on parole. They listened intently from the back row of benches in the courtroom as Clyne Harradence fired questions at Scraba. When Scraba, in response to one of Harradence's questions, said he was only following orders from his bosses, McLaren shook his head and told his wife. "He's lying."

Scraba took a drink from the glass of water as he waited for Harradence's next question. "The devil made me do it," Harradence said as he advanced on Scraba. He stopped in front of the witness box, less than an arm's length from Scraba's face.

"Those big bad MLAs." "The MLAs wanted me to do it," Scraba fired back. He said the politicians would like people to believe they had no knowledge of what was going on, but they did know and many of them got cash through the use of phony invoices. He said not only did the MLAs know they were breaking the guidelines, they "knew how to manipulate the system to get whatever they wanted."

When asked whether he gave any cash to Sherwin Petersen, Scraba replied that he couldn't recall giving Petersen any cash, but he added that the former MLA bought a video camera and a computer using phony invoices through his Communication Allowance. The invoice for the camera was marked "computer rental." During his testimony, Scraba also said that Petersen was among four politicians who had told him in 1987 to set up the numbered companies to collect money from members' Communication Allowances. He said he took his instructions from those same politicians, including Petersen.

But Clyne Harradence wasn't buying Scraba's explanations. He called John Scraba an "inveterate liar as a swindler has to be." And he described the scheme set up in the PC caucus office as John Scraba's personal money-laundering scam. He accused the Crown of giving Scraba a deal for being the "rat" against MLAs. Scraba countered that the Crown had never backed off his case, not "one iota." He reminded Harradence that at his trial, Crown prosecutor Eric Neufeld had pushed for three years in prison.

When John Scraba walked out of a Regina courtroom after testifying at Sherwin Petersen's trial, an RCMP officer, the woman who had replaced Sergeant John Leitch on Project Fiddle, called to him as he headed down a long hallway toward the door on the west end of the building. She met him halfway and together they walked back down the hallway where no one could hear their conversation. They talked for a few minutes and then the police officer walked away. Scraba headed for the door and out into the June sunshine.

Later, sipping a beer in a hotel lounge a couple of blocks west of the courthouse, Scraba said the police officer wanted him to give a statement regarding the Martensville account.

Scraba said he told the officer he wanted to talk with a lawyer first, but he said he had no intention of giving another statement to the police on anything. "They got what they are getting from me," he said as he lifted his glass. He said he felt like he was on a leash and whenever the police wanted him they yanked and he came. "When I leave Regina I push it out of my head." He said if he didn't get a break from it all he'd go crazy. He estimated that his latest appearance was his nineteenth time in the witness box.

The former radio announcer now worked with an entertainment company in Edmonton as a disc jockey, playing music at weddings, banquets, and dances. He knew very well that he was in the bad books of many of his former Tory colleagues. People he had once chatted with freely in the corridors of power now wouldn't even acknowledge him and if they did, it was usually with a dirty look. They called him the snitch, liar, thief, con-artist, and turncoat who had spilled the beans in an attempt to save his own hide. As long as the trials continued, Scraba would not be off the hook.

When it was Sherwin Petersen's turn to sit in the witness box in his own defence, he told Justice Archambault that he didn't know about the fraud scheme when he worked in the caucus office and that he had trusted Scraba to do the right thing. He denied being part of a group that oversaw the pooling of communication money. He said caucus simply asked his opinion on the pool from time to time. And he said he didn't know about the numbered companies set up in the caucus office either. He admitted he received $3,000 in cash from John Scraba, but he said it was reimbursement for a faulty computer. When Crown prosecutor Sharon Pratchler asked him if he had ever wondered where Scraba got the money from, he replied, "I never gave it a second thought."

In the end, despite the lengthy delays, the accusations of misconduct, and the thousands of dollars spent on lawyers, the judge accepted only some of Sherwin Petersen's testimony. On July 15, he found the former MLA guilty of one count of fraud over $5,000, but he acquitted him on the other count of fraud over $5,000 and on the charge of conspiracy with John Scraba to commit fraud. Justice Archambault found that Petersen personally obtained cash, computer equipment, and a video camera valued at $9,285 from the caucus office fraud scheme. He said he didn't believe Petersen when he testified that he didn't know Scraba had submitted false MLA expense allowance claims on his behalf. He said that Petersen's explanation defied logic and his sweeping denials lacked credibility. "I am confident beyond any doubt that Petersen was fully aware of the fraudulent means used," Justice Archambault said in his ruling. He added that while he had his suspicions about whether Petersen had knowledge of a scheme to defraud the government of more than $837,000, he was giving him the benefit of the doubt.

At the sentencing hearing on August 25, 1997, Clyne Harradence told the court that Petersen had been "financially ruined" by the proceedings. He said an absolutely honourable man had been through bankruptcy, suffered a heart attack, been "vilified by the media," and now had to supplement his farming income by working as a hand on oil rigs. "He has had his whole life destroyed."

The judge accepted Harradence's recommendation for a conditional discharge. Petersen was ordered to do 240 hours of community service work and to pay restitution of $9,285. He was also placed on probation for three years. In the end, once he completed the probation period, Petersen would not have a criminal record. In his comments during sentencing, the judge said he believed the conditional discharge was appropriate, in part, because Petersen was "duped." He said, "I find that Petersen was dragged by the current." He added that he should have known better.

The Crown appealed to the Saskatchewan Court of Appeal, arguing that Petersen should have been sent to jail or at least been given a period of electronic monitoring. The appeal was rejected. Sherwin Petersen spent his 240 hours of community service work cleaning sewers and repairing waterworks.

The Courthouse Parade
Continues

Michael McCafferty, the speechwriter who had been a Crown witness against Michael Hopfner, was the next Tory to face a judge. In January 1997, he had been charged with defrauding Saskatchewan taxpayers of $36,657. Shortly after the charges were laid, some of his friends set up a Michael McCafferty legal fund at a Regina branch of the Bank of Montreal. They placed an ad in newspapers in Regina and Saskatoon. The Bank of Montreal responded by placing an ad in the same newspapers stating it wouldn't accept contributions for the McCafferty fund. In a written statement, the bank said it wasn't asked to sponsor a fund for McCafferty. It said it only sponsored funds for registered, non-profit charity groups or associations with legal status. McCafferty got upset and accused the Bank of Montreal of labelling him a criminal before he had even had his day in court. He sent over 150 letters to family and friends across the country asking for money to help him pay his legal bills.

On October 6, 1997, the day his preliminary hearing was scheduled to begin, Michael McCafferty pleaded guilty. And the day he entered his plea, he also read a prepared statement into reporters' microphones on the courthouse steps. "This morning is a very dark and sad day in my life," he began. "It would have been very easy for me to keep on hiding behind the excuse that I was used and pressured by two members of the Legislature into doing wrong. That is not right. In my heart, I know that I did wrong and there is no excuse for doing wrong and I am very, very sorry and I am very ashamed. I've hurt my wife and my children. I've let down my friends." His voice cracked but he continued.

"And I've been part of a political scandal that has put a very black cloud over politics in Saskatchewan. In my prayers, I've asked God for his forgiveness. In my heart I hope that the people of Saskatchewan, the good and decent people, the taxpayers, would find it in their hearts to forgive me. And to them I would say I am very, very sorry. And please forgive me. Thank you."

In responding to reporters' questions following the statement, McCafferty refused to point fingers. When asked whether he thought former premier Grant Devine had any idea of what was going on, McCafferty replied that Devine was a "good and decent man" who had been betrayed by a lot of very corrupt people. As for his own actions, McCafferty said, "I did wrong in terms of doing something wrong in the system and an error in judgement. But I honestly didn't believe that I set out with [the] intent to steal or defraud the taxpayers of Saskatchewan." McCafferty said he received a share of the cash he helped two MLAs get from their Communication Allowances.

In handing down the sentence on December 16, 1997, Provincial Court Judge Dennis Fenwick said, "Mr. McCafferty was used and abused by those with more power and prestige." The judge went on to say that he was firmly convinced that "Mr. McCafferty should not be sentenced to a term of imprisonment." The judge also took into account McCafferty's physical and psychiatric state in assessing a penalty. Evidence was produced in court that McCafferty suffered from clinical depression, diabetes, asthma, and sleep apnea. McCafferty was drawing a disability pension and had not worked since he became ill in late 1990. The judge said he also thought that McCafferty had shown genuine remorse. He sentenced the forty-six-year-old former Tory speechwriter to one year to be served in the community and ordered him to do sixty hours of community service.

Commenting on the impact of Project Fiddle on his family, McCafferty said they were devastated. His daughter, who was in grade 8 when he was charged, had students at her school say, "Your dad's a crook. Your dad's one of those rotten, dirty Tory crooks." His father once told him that all you take to your grave is your reputation. He said he had shamed his wife, his children, his friends, and his father's memory. Over the years he often dreamed that one day he would run for a political office but he now realized that would never happen. He had to settle for reading and writing about politics, especially on the Internet. Michael McCafferty has his own web page and it's all about politics.

While Michael McCafferty's trial was in progress, another Tory, John Scraba's former friend and colleague Harry Baker was also on the hot seat. Harry Baker went before Court of Queen's Bench Justice Eugene Scheibel on November 12, 1997. The fifty-nine-year-old farmer and businessman was charged with fraudulently obtaining $22,545 by submitting false claims on his MLA Communication Allowance. During interviews with the RCMP when the investigation first started, Baker admitted to receiving cash from John Scraba, but he said the money was to cover legitimate expenses he had paid out of his own pocket. The police investigators believed Baker received three $1,000 bills and some $100 bills from John Scraba.

Baker, a self-described wheeler-dealer businessman, was the MLA for Biggar from 1982 until 1991, when he was defeated at the polls. Baker was born and raised on a farm in Saskatchewan. He left school when he was eight to help on the family farm because his father was crippled. He later moved to Edmonton, where he ran a gas bar and then a furniture store. When he moved back to Saskatchewan, he opened his own furniture store in Saskatoon. He then sold it and set up a construction company to build houses. He was now back farming and was a part owner with his wife in a fabric store in Saskatoon.

Before the trial began, Baker's lawyer, Rod Donlevy, made several unsuccessful attempts to have the charges thrown out. He claimed the RCMP search warrants weren't proper and that there had been too many delays in getting the case to trial. The trial had been postponed twice since Baker had been charged two and a half years earlier. Baker also failed in his attempt to have the trial moved to Saskatoon. Baker, who had elected to be tried by judge and jury, argued that it would be more difficult to get a fair trial in Regina because of publicity about the Tory fraud scandal in the Queen City. When he lost the bid to have the trial moved, he decided to go with a judge alone.

In the courtroom, Sergeant John Leitch laid out the Crown's

case using his laptop computer, invoices, cheques, and cash deposits for Harry Baker's personal bank account. He introduced evidence to show that Baker and his wife made cash deposits to their bank accounts totalling more than $10,800 in 1989 and 1990. The deposits included three $1,000 bills, sixty-seven $100 bills, and fifteen $50 bills. The serial numbers on the $1,000 bills were in sequence with numbers on the $1,000 bills found in the safety deposit boxes.

When it was John Scraba's turn to testify, he told the judge that he gave envelopes of cash to Baker. "I would deliver the money to him with just the two of us in the office," he said. He said he gave Baker cash at least twice when he requested money for constituency expenses, using phony invoices to get the money.

Harry Baker said all the claims he submitted on his allowances were for legitimate expenses. Baker, who liked to gamble and was a frequent visitor to casinos in Saskatoon and Regina, told police the $1,000 bills that were deposited in the personal bank accounts must have come from winnings at the blackjack table. His lawyer called witnesses, including a blackjack dealer at the casino in Saskatoon, to talk about the former MLA's gambling habits. The witnesses described Baker as a progressive gambler who would even bet on the timing of raindrops hitting the ground. He was known as a high-stakes gambler who liked to play the blackjack tables with the $25 to $100 limits. He also played the horses. He owned a racehorse and bet on him sometimes and he bought lots of lottery tickets. He even had his own system for picking the numbers.

When Baker testified in his own defence, he said he won more than $22,000 in the 6/49 lottery in 1988 and over the next four years won thousands of dollars on at least six occasions. As for blackjack, Baker said he knew when a table was cold or hot. And he said he'd had some big winnings. One time at a casino in Regina, he was "on a roll" and made more than $5,000 at the blackjack tables. He also liked to play high-stakes poker games at private clubs. During those games, a big pot would be in the neighbourhood of two thousand dollars.

Harry Baker also tried to convince the judge that he was a

successful businessman and had no reason to defraud taxpayers of a few thousand dollars. In an attempt to prove he was an honest man with the taxpayers' best interests at heart, he spilt the beans on what he considered to be some shady dealings that went on in the Devine government when he was an MLA.

The former caucus chair had insider information on the Martensville account. Harry Baker was caucus chair when Katzman first asked for the money. He said word got around that Katzman wanted to clean out the caucus bank account. As caucus chair, he let it be known that he was having no part of it, and he refused to cut Katzman a cheque, even though Katzman met with him a couple of times and told him it was standard practice and that he had done it a couple of times before. A few weeks after his meetings with Katzman, he learned through the media that he had been replaced as caucus chair.

Baker also described a plan to sell a provincial government-owned company to a bunch of Tories as "really scuzzy." He said that in 1988 he began hearing rumours of a plan to sell Prairie Malt cheap to a company called Producers Pipelines Incorporated, which was partly owned by some high-ranking Conservatives. Prairie Malt, which made malt for the brewing industry, was a major employer in the town of Biggar, about one hundred kilometres west of Saskatoon. Baker was the MLA for the area at the time. The plant employed about seventy people. The private company had been taken over by the Progressive Conservative government in the early 1980s when it fell on hard times.

Baker said when he first heard of the deal being put together for some Tories, he got a friend to buy shares in Producers Pipelines, so he could get a list of the shareholders. The list showed that prominent Tories owned the majority of the shares. Baker said he then tracked down Grant Devine and told him that there was a deal in the works to sell Prairie Malt for $19 million—$9 million less than the company was worth— to a bunch of Tories. He told Devine he would quit his job and go public if the deal wasn't cancelled. He said Devine quickly made a telephone call and called him back to say the deal was dead. In the end, the province's Crown Investments Corporation sold Prairie Malt to Schreier Malting Company of Wisconsin and the Saskatchewan Wheat Pool in September 1989.

Even though Baker's stories of alleged backroom deals made good headlines for the media, they didn't seem to count much in the courtroom. Crown prosecutor Sharon Pratchler continued to point out that her case lay in the stacks of cheques, invoices, and bank records that Sergeant John Leitch produced with ease in the courtroom. Baker and his lawyer, Rod Donlevy, had trouble convincing the judge that the $1,000 bills came from his gambling pursuits.

On February 19, 1998, Harry Baker, who had recently turned sixty, was found guilty of fraud. He was given a one-year conditional sentence and a curfew that required him to stay on his farm east of Saskatoon for the first four months of his sentence. In addition, he was ordered to repay the $22,545 he had received by submitting phony invoices.

In handing down the sentence, Justice Scheibel said that MLAs should face the same sentences as ordinary citizens who are convicted of defrauding the public. He noted that most of them are given a jail sentence. But the judge said Baker's sentence had to be in line with those handed the other Tories who were convicted. All but four of them up to this point had received some combination of conditional discharges, probation, fines, and restitution orders. Lorne McLaren, John Scraba, John Gerich, and Michael Hopfner were the only ones who had been sent to jail.

A couple of months later, Bob Pickering, another former Tory cabinet minister, found himself facing Provincial Court Judge Dennis Fenwick. Pickering, a thin man who always looked as though nothing really bothered him, was retired and spent most winters in Arizona. In January 1997, the sixty-four-year-old former politician had been charged with defrauding taxpayers by submitting nearly $27,000 worth of false MLA expense claims. The Crown alleged he kept the money for personal use.

Bob Pickering was first elected to the Saskatchewan Legislature in 1978 and served in Grant Devine's cabinet from 1982 to 1985 as minister of rural affairs and parks and renewable resources. He was dropped from the cabinet in 1985.

Pickering was re-elected in 1986. The former MLA for the rural riding of Bengough-Milestone didn't run in the 1991 provincial election. The Crown alleged that Bob Pickering got help to commit fraud from both John Scraba and Michael McCafferty. His trial began on May 4, 1998.

In the courtroom, Pickering's lawyer, Gordon Kuski, argued his client was an "unwitting, innocent victim of a fraternity of fraudsters." He accused Scraba and McCafferty of preying upon his client. When all the evidence was in, the judge described the Crown's case as compelling and Pickering's story as highly suspect, but he said he still had doubts. "The court still must be convinced beyond a reasonable doubt before a conviction can be rendered," Judge Fenwick announced. On May 26 he found Bob Pickering not guilty. Bob Pickering was the fourth Tory to be cleared. Outside the courthouse, he told reporters the ordeal had taught him one thing, "Not to trust anybody."

Beattie Martin, a former broadcaster and politician who now sold houses, was patiently waiting for his turn in court. He was anxious to get it over with. In January 1997, Martin had been charged with one count of fraud over $5,000. The RCMP claimed that he had received $23,410 by submitting false expense claims through his Communication Allowance.

Martin admitted that he had received cash from John Scraba. He said he used it to buy a camera, to pay for his annual membership at the Regina Golf Club ($980), and to purchase his Roughriders' season tickets (about $400). At earlier court hearings for some of his colleagues, he said he didn't see anything wrong with what he did. He said taking constituents to football games and taking people golfing is a good way of entertaining them on behalf of the government.

Beattie Martin was elected to the Legislature in the constituency of Regina South in 1986. He was appointed to the cabinet in the fall of 1989 as the minister for the family. He was also given responsibilities for seniors, culture, multiculturalism, and recreation.

Just before his trial was to start, Martin worked out a deal with the Crown prosecutor's office. On March 11, 1999, he pleaded guilty to a lesser charge of fraud under $5,000. He, too, was given a conditional discharge, placed on probation for a year, and ordered to do 200 hours of community service work. Court of Queen's Bench Justice Catherine Dawson also ordered him to pay back $2,900. "My conscience is clear," he told reporters as he left the courthouse. "I paid it back and I feel good about that. It was a mistake and I admit it."

The Senator's Judgement Day

Eric Berntson, once one of the most formidable politicians in Saskatchewan, was in deep trouble. When Sergeant John Leitch sifted through evidence to build a case against Bob Andrew, he found more than he was looking for. Some of the documents he scanned led him to believe that Senator Eric Berntson may have been obtaining cash from his MLA Communication Allowance. His interest was piqued when he found a cheque for $5,000 written on the account of Dome Advertising and addressed to Berriedale Management Incorporated, a company that Leitch recognized as belonging to Berntson. Berriedale Management was set up in Estevan (Grant Devine's constituency) in 1982, the same year the Conservatives came to power. Berntson was listed as the sole owner. It was registered as a resource, exploration, and development company. The company was dropped from the province's register of companies in 1992.

As Sergeant John Leitch dug deeper into Dome's records, many of which had been placed in storage after the agency went out of business in the early 1990s, he came across a second cheque to Berriedale for $8,450. Leitch also found evidence of a third transaction between Dome and Berriedale. By the time his search was over, he had gathered a three-foot stack of bank records and computer printouts that was to form the basis for fraud charges against both Eric Berntson and Bob Andrew.

The fifty-six-year-old Berntson was the most prominent of all the Tories charged in Project Fiddle. He had been born in Oxbow, Saskatchewan, May 16, 1941. He quit school in grade 9 because, as he later recalled, "I'd had enough of that silliness." He completed his grade 12 in Halifax so he could join the armed forces. He served with the Canadian Navy and Canadian Air

Force for eight years. When he left the armed forces he moved to Calgary, where he worked nights in electronic data processing for National Cash Register. He attended university during the day, taking classes in pre-law, pre-medicine, and political science, but he never did finish a degree. He eventually returned to Saskatchewan and began farming near Carievale, a small town in the southeastern part of the province.

Eric Berntson was first elected to the Saskatchewan Legislature in the traditionally Conservative rural constituency of Souris-Cannington in 1975, and again in 1978, 1982, and 1986. He was deputy premier and government house leader from May 8, 1982, until October 3, 1989; minister of agriculture from May 8, 1982, until July 15, 1983; minister of economic development and trade from July 15, 1983, until December 16, 1985; and minister of economic development and tourism from October 3, 1989, to March 16, 1990. He served on the boards of most Crown corporations during his term in government.

The shrewd politician joked that he was railroaded into politics because he had been "the most vocal guy in the local coffee shop." Some of his colleagues in the Tory Party said Berntson was the administrative head of the provincial government when the Tories came to power, while Grant Devine was the front man, the speechmaker, and the media star. Berntson resigned his seat in the provincial government on July 19, 1990. On September 27, 1990, he was summoned to the Senate by Brian Mulroney. He was one of Mulroney's infamous "GST senators," added to the Senate to ensure the Goods and Services Tax became law. In January 1994 he was appointed deputy leader of the opposition in the Senate.

Eric Berntson, the man who was deputy premier for close to eight of the nine years Grant Devine's Conservatives were in power in Saskatchewan, was charged with fraud in January 1997. Police alleged he had defrauded the public of $68,055, using three different methods on three different expense allowances: his Communication Allowance, his Constituency Office and Services Allowance, and his Constituency Secretarial Allowance. Berntson also faced a charge of breach of trust and a charge of fraud for allegedly assisting in the diversion of

$125,000 from the PC caucus account to the Progressive Conservative Party of Saskatchewan in early 1987. On this last count, he was charged jointly with Don Pringle, a former executive director with the Conservative Party of Saskatchewan and a special advisor to Grant Devine. Pringle and Berntson had talked with former caucus chair Lorne McLaren about transferring $125,000 from the PC caucus account to the PC Party. After their chat, McLaren handed over the money.

In January 1997, the senator's lawyer, Clyne Harradence, complained about "leaks" in the RCMP. Harradence had received three telephone calls from reporters the day before the RCMP announced at a press conference that six Tories (including Eric Berntson) were being charged. "Somebody whispered in somebody's ear that there were going to be charges laid," he told a reporter.

When the senator was first charged with fraud, the Reform and New Democratic parties attacked him in the House of Commons. They called for him to resign from his duties in the Conservative caucus until the charges had been dealt with. Berntson bent to the pressure and stopped doing the duties of deputy leader of the opposition, but he kept the job and the salary, confident that he would be exonerated during the court process. He continued to attend sessions of the Senate.

Eric Berntson had already weathered a number of political storms. One concerned his involvement with the computer translation company GigaText. When Berntson was deputy premier, he welcomed the company into the province. The Saskatchewan government, prompted by a Supreme Court ruling, had just decided to translate some of its laws into French, so GigaText's promised translation services were welcomed with open arms. The province invested $4 million in GigaText for 25 percent of the shares.

GigaText used Saskatchewan taxpayers' money to pay $2.9 million for twenty computers an independent auditor valued at just $39,000. Deputy Premier Eric Berntson defended the purchase, claiming that the province got "value for the dollar when GigaText bought the computers." But later, when Japanese businessman Takayuka Tsuru sued GigaText owner

Guy Montpetit, it was learned that Montpetit had pocketed a large chunk of the money his company had received for the computers. Tsuru had loaned Montpetit $39 million for a factory that would manufacture silicon chips. Five months after the start-up of GigaText, most of the province's $4 million had been spent and the provincial government had little to show for its investment. When the government finally admitted there was serious trouble, it loaned GigaText another $1.25 million. The government eventually took over the company in March 1989. The Tories would invest another $75,000 before shutting down GigaText in November 1989.

Then there was the case of Cameco. In 1990, after he left provincial politics, Eric Berntson worked as a consultant to Cameco, which had been formed in the fall of 1988 when Saskatchewan Mining Development Corporation (SMDC), a provincial crown corporation, merged with the federal Crown corporation Eldorado Nuclear. Cameco operated a number of uranium mines in Saskatchewan. Berntson was familiar with Cameco because in early 1988 he had been minister in charge of SMDC when it was still a Crown Corporation. Cameco paid Berntson $355,000 as a consultant for "strategic planning assistance" and for help in discussions with the provincial government.

As a result of an article published in The Globe and Mail on February 6, 1993, which linked Berntson, Cameco, and a law firm in Saskatchewan, the Law Society of Saskatchewan instigated a series of disciplinary hearings into the relationship between Cameco, Senator Berntson, and the law firm. The lawyers were charged with conduct unbecoming a lawyer. On October 27, 1995, the RCMP's Commercial Crime Section issued a news release to confirm it, too, was investigating business practices that took place during 1990 and 1991 between Cameco, the law firm, and Berntson. There were allegations of kickbacks and influence peddling. The Law Society pursued the matter until January 1996, when a justice with the provincial Court of Queen's Bench ruled that its investigations had gone "completely off the rails" and that the hearing had become a substitute police investigation. The Law Society did not challenge the judge's ruling, and neither the RCMP investigation nor the Law Society's disciplinary hearings went anywhere.

With the Cameco business behind him, Senator Eric Berntson could now turn his full attention to fending off allegations surrounding Project Fiddle. A preliminary hearing for the senator and Don Pringle began in provincial court in Regina on October 20, 1997. The two men were jointly charged with diverting $125,000 from the PC caucus account to the Progressive Conservative Party of Saskatchewan in early 1987. Berntson was also facing allegations of fraud concerning false expense claims on three of his MLA allowances.

A biting autumn wind cut through the downtown streets of the Queen City as the two former colleagues arrived at the provincial courthouse for their hearing. Clyne Harradence, who had represented Berntson during the law society's investigations, was once again at Berntson's side. Pringle had hired Mike Megaw, a newcomer to Project Fiddle, to handle his defence. Megaw had been Gerry Muirhead's lawyer, so he had some experience defending a politician who had been charged with fraud.

A few days into the hearing, and a few hours before it was expected to wrap up, Harradence acknowledged that the Crown had provided sufficient evidence for the judge to order Berntson to stand trial on the charge of fraud involving expense claims. Provincial Court Judge Bruce Henning reserved his decision for both Berntson and Pringle on the charges connected with the $125,000 given to the PC Party.

The following month, seven days before Christmas, Don Pringle was cleared of any wrongdoing. In his decision, the judge stated that "if theft occurred it was committed by [Lorne] McLaren who made the cheque and sent the funds to the [PC] Party." McLaren claimed that he was just following orders from Pringle and Berntson when he wrote the cheque for $125,000 and handed it over to the PC Party. The judge found that there was no evidence to show that Pringle had deliberately deceived McLaren. Eric Berntson, however, had to wait another month for the judge to decide whether he, too, would be cleared of any wrongdoing in connection with the $125,000.

Don Pringle was beaming as he walked through the main door of the courthouse. During the court hearing he had avoided reporters, but now he was eager to talk. "It was never my intent on any part to do anything illegal," he told a couple of reporters as the three of them huddled against a biting prairie wind on a landing just outside the courthouse door. "This has certainly been a nightmare for me and my family. I think it has devastated my reputation here in the province. My parents and my family have had a long and distinguished [history of] service to this province. And this charge has . . . unfairly tarnished that record. And from the beginning, four and a half, five years ago, I told the police what had happened and [they] chose to believe someone else in this matter. And that other version was not substantiated on the stand, so I am very pleased that His Honour, based on the evidence, chose to dismiss the charges against me." Pringle, who had resigned from his job in Edmonton, Alberta, when he was first charged, said, "[I am going to] restore my reputation, my career, and my life."

A month later, Judge Henning dismissed the fraud charge against Eric Berntson involving the $125,000, but ordered him to stand trial on the breach of trust charge related to the same money. In his ruling, the judge stated that the difference between Don Pringle and Eric Berntson was that Berntson was an MLA and a member of the PC caucus, whereas Pringle was not and that was why he let the breach of trust charge against Berntson go ahead. The senator faced another fraud charge, which alleged he used false expense claims submitted to three different expense allowances to get cash through one of the numbered companies John Scraba set up in the PC caucus office, through Dome Advertising, and through Berriedale Management.

A few months later, Clyne Harradence withdrew as Berntson's lawyer, saying he didn't have the time to handle the case. The senator then hired Mike Megaw, the lawyer who had successfully defended Don Pringle. The senator's trial was expected to start in the fall of 1998, but before it could proceed, the case became bogged down in questions about whether NDP MLAs had also abused their allowances during the 1980s.

Mike Megaw went to court on December 30, 1998, seeking expense allowance records for NDP and Liberal MLAs between April 1985 and December 1991. The request included documents for NDP Premier Roy Romanow and former premier Allan Blakeney, as well as former Liberal leaders Ralph Goodale (who had gone on to become a federal cabinet minister) and Lynda Haverstock. Megaw argued that the records were pertinent to Berntson's defence. He said that with access to the records, he could determine whether there was a standard operating procedure used to submit claims on MLA expense allowances. He said if Berntson had used the same procedure, it would be harder for the Crown to prove he had intent to defraud the public. Megaw denied that his requests had "political overtones," since he was seeking information on both NDP and Liberal MLAs.

The Crown, the clerk of the Legislature, and the provincial Finance Department turned down Mike Megaw's request for the information. Court of Queen's Bench Justice Frank Gerein, however, agreed with Megaw that the records he was after were likely relevant to the trial. He gave Megaw a few days to notify MLAs that he wanted to take a look at the documents and said those who objected would be given the opportunity to make their case in court on January 8, 1999. The issue sparked another round of political sniping and new accusations of wrongdoing. Some of the current and former MLAs covered by the request didn't have a problem with it. One former NDP MLA who objected came to court to argue his case. He said his only concern was that handing over the documents would reveal the identities of his former constituency assistants. He noted that some of them were working in the public service and if the government ever changed, he feared they would be fired because of their previous association with the NDP.

A group of thirty-eight New Democrats, including Roy Romanow and Allan Blakeney, hired a lawyer in an attempt to block the request. Their lawyer questioned the motivation behind the request. He argued that the defence wanted the records in hopes they might stumble across something useful. He argued that his clients were not concerned about the release of the information, but merely wanted to ensure their rights were considered before the documents were handed over. Justice Gerein ordered that Mike Megaw be given access to the records for sixty-eight past and present MLAs, most of them New Democrats.

Eric Berntson's trial began on January 11, 1999, about two years after he was charged. Sergeant John Leitch, armed with his trusty computer, his financial spreadsheets, boxes of documents, an overhead projector, and television monitors, was the Crown's key witness. The RCMP officer went through the evidence to support the charge that the former deputy premier had defrauded the public of $68,055. Berntson was accused of drawing $26,320 from his Communication Allowance: $18,450 using invoices submitted by Dome Advertising and $7,870 using invoices submitted to John Scraba for payment via the numbered companies. He was also accused of using false invoices from Berriedale Management to draw $31,046 from his Constituency Secretarial Allowance and $10,689 from his Constituency Office and Services Allowance.

Leitch started with the evidence that Berntson had used false invoices provided by Dome Advertising to obtain $18,450 from his MLA Communication Allowance. The RCMP officer testified that in June 1987, Berntson had submitted a $5,000 expense claim on his Communication Allowance, supported by an invoice from Dome for communications consulting. The senator claimed he had already paid the bill and asked the Legislative Assembly to reimburse him directly. However, Leitch says his search uncovered no evidence of a $5,000 payment from Berntson to Dome. According to Leitch, another bill for $8,450 was handled in a similar fashion. This time the money went directly to Dome, and Dome then issued a cheque for $8,450 to Berriedale Management Incorporated, Berntson's Estevan company. The police sergeant went on to say that Berntson followed the same procedure in October 1989, when he submitted a $5,000 claim for a communications strategy from Dome. Leitch says the $5,000 cheque related to that transaction, signed by Dome president Phil Kershaw, sparked the investigation into Berntson's dealings with the company.

Phil Kershaw, the former co-owner and president of Dome, testified that Berntson called him some time in the late 1980s and asked him to generate a $5,000 invoice for communications consulting. Kershaw said once the bill was paid by the Legislative Assembly, he was to write a cheque to Berriedale

Management. Kershaw and Dome's former officer manager told the court they were unaware of any work being performed in relation to the invoice. Kershaw also told the court that Berntson never asked him to perform any work in relation to the invoice and never told him what the transaction involved. Kershaw admitted he didn't ask any questions. In response to a question from the Crown prosecutor Sharon Pratchler, Kershaw said he had the utmost respect for Berntson and if the deputy premier wanted something done, he was glad to offer his assistance.

During cross-examination by the defence, both Kershaw and the former office manager admitted that although they didn't recall having done work for Berntson, they didn't have intimate knowledge of what other company executives might have done for him. The advertising company's records showing what services had been done for individual clients had been destroyed when Dome closed in 1994.

In Saskatchewan, Phil Kershaw is probably best known as a former president of the Saskatchewan Roughriders and chair of the Canadian Football League. When he testified at Berntson's trial, he was working as a sports consultant in Ottawa. Outside the courtroom, Kershaw told reporters that he didn't relish having to testify against the former deputy premier. He said he thought very highly of Senator Berntson, "I think he's a fine person individually and I think he provided a lot of service for Saskatchewan over the years."

In court, Crown prosecutor Sharon Pratchler argued that Berntson used Dome as a vehicle to obtain cash from his MLA Communication Allowance "because he was broke." When reporters asked her why Kershaw wasn't charged after admitting he wrote a phony invoice, she replied that Kershaw, along with a lot of other innocent bystanders, was deceived as part of the overall scheme. She added that the former Dome president had relied on the integrity of the member who was making the request.

The Crown also alleged that Eric Berntson got caucus communications director John Scraba to submit two bogus invoices to the Legislature using the numbered companies and then pay him the $7,870 proceeds. When Scraba came to the witness box, he told the judge that the former deputy premier approached him shortly before his 1990 resignation from provincial politics and asked Scraba to help him obtain cash from his MLA Communication Allowance. Scraba said he prepared two invoices, using one of the companies he had set up in the caucus office, and submitted them, along with expense claims signed by Berntson, to the Legislature for payment. When the bills were paid, he handed Berntson an envelope containing nearly $8,000 in cash. At the time, Berntson was having significant money trouble and had run up an overdraft of about $50,000.

Later, talking with reporters outside the courthouse, John Scraba, dressed in a dark suit and wearing a tie and sporting sunglasses, showed no sympathy for the senator. "When it was told and shown to me without a shadow of a doubt that what I did was wrong, I sucked it up and I took my medicine. Others continue, as they did in government, to stick their heads in the sand and blame others for their actions. . . . All I know is that my life has been on hold for almost a decade and I'm ready to resume it," he said as he walked away. "And that is exactly what I am going to do."

Senator Eric Berntson sat quietly next to his lawyer as a parade of witnesses tied him into the biggest political scandal in Saskatchewan's history. During the trial, his wife, Joan, sat in the courtroom taking notes. And during recess times the senator spent the time talking with his lawyer or his wife, or both.

The Crown also alleged that Berntson made false claims on his Constituency Secretarial Allowance to obtain $31,046. As he did with the previous allegations, Sergeant John Leitch laid the paper trail from the witness box. In 1988, the MLAs' Constituency Secretarial Allowances were doubled so that they could keep their offices open full time. According to Leitch, instead of increasing the hours of the secretary in his Carlyle office, Berntson obtained the money—an extra $1,000 a month—for himself using invoices from Berriedale Management. Leitch testified that Berntson submitted invoices to the Legislature indicating that his constituency secretary received an extra $860 to $1,000 a month. When it was the secretary's turn to testify, she acknowledged that her signature appeared at the bottom of the invoices, but she said that someone else had filled in the rest of the information.

Defence lawyer Mike Megaw countered that Berntson was entitled to claim the money to compensate his spouses for secretarial duties they performed in the home. Neither of his wives worked out of the constituency office, but under the rules, an MLA is allowed to hire his or her spouse as a secretary.

When Eric Berntson's first wife, Jean Howell, was called as a defence witness, she testified that she never expected taxpayers to pay her a salary for answering her husband's telephone calls and opening his mail. Berntson and Howell had separated in October 1988 after having been married for just over twenty years. Joan Berntson, the senator's second wife, testified that while she didn't receive any direct payment for helping her husband, the money he received benefitted her indirectly because it was used for such things as keeping the furnace running and the lights on. Joan began living with Eric Berntson in June 1989 and the couple married in January the following year. When asked by Crown prosecutor Sharon Pratchler whether she had ever declared any of these payments on her income tax, Joan Berntson replied that she had not. She added that if she had known then what she knew now, she certainly would have. Later during Eric Berntson's testimony, Crown prosecutor Sharon Pratchler asked him if he ever told his wives that if they stopped answering the telephone, they would lose their benefits and have to leave home. Berntson replied, "That's a ridiculous suggestion."

The Crown also alleged that the former deputy premier made false claims on his Constituency Office and Services Allowance to obtain $10,689. Sergeant John Leitch produced documents showing that after all the bills had been paid for the operation of his constituency office, Eric Berntson submitted phony invoices from Berriedale, his Estevan company, to claim the remaining amount in his Constituency Office and Services Allowance. According to the rules of the Legislature, MLAs could set up management companies to run their constituency offices, but the companies had to incur expenditures in order to make claims, and Berriedale, it seems, had no expenses to show for the extra money that Berntson claimed.

As for the $125,000 that was taken out of the PC caucus account and given to the Progressive Conservative Party of Saskatchewan in early 1987, the Crown alleged that Eric Berntson played an instrumental role in that illegal act. The caucus chair at the time, Lorne McLaren, said he issued the cheque to the party at the request of Berntson and Don Pringle. McLaren said he understood it was a loan, but party officials said they assumed it was to help pay for polling the party arranged to be done for the PC caucus. According to the legislative clerk, caucus grants could be used for polling as long as the polls were done for the caucus. The polling in question was done in the months leading up to the 1986 provincial election. The Crown alleged that the contract for polling was between the PC Party and Toronto-based Decima Research and that there was nothing in the contracts to indicate that any work had been done for the PC caucus.

Don Pringle, who had earlier been cleared of any wrongdoing in connection with the transfer of the money, described the transfer as an "afterthought" since the polling bills had already been paid without any discussion of the PC caucus paying a share. He admitted in court that it was obviously a "sloppy" way of doing business since no documentation explaining the transaction had been prepared. During cross-examination by the defence, the RCMP officer who investigated the transaction told the court that he might have halted his investigation if he had known that caucuses were allowed to spend money on public-opinion polling.

At Michael Hopfner's trial in October 1996, Eric Berntson had testified that he told Lorne McLaren to make sure the payment would be proper before he issued the cheque. "I suggested that if they [caucus] could pay for the research that was done on their behalf and if they could discover whether or not it was appropriate to do so, they should do it." At the time, Berntson testified that Don Pringle approached him with the idea of getting caucus to help pay for party polling. It was just following the 1986 provincial election and the party was short on cash. Eric Berntson testified that he and Pringle walked over to the caucus office and discussed the matter with McLaren. "The total conversation I would say, took less than two minutes," Berntson said at Hopfner's trial. "After that conversation I have no knowledge of what happened, whether or not the cheque ever went over."

According to a party worker who testified at Eric Berntson's trial, Lorne McLaren told her to keep the matter "circumspect" because other caucus members might not agree with the payment. She said she thought it was a grant and became concerned when the party president asked her to prepare a letter that referred to the payment as a loan. Another party worker, who was assigned to write the letter, said she was told by McLaren that when she finished typing the letter, she should "totally forget that you typed it and never tell anyone." The worker said after she typed the letter, she threw away the typewriter ribbon as instructed. McLaren said he never told anyone to forget about writing a letter or to throw away a typewriter ribbon. McLaren was scheduled to testify at Eric Berntson's trial but couldn't because he was in hospital. The judge allowed the Crown to play a recording of McLaren's testimony at Berntson's preliminary hearing, which had taken place fourteen months earlier.

Gwenn Ronyk, the legislative clerk, testified that the Tory caucus was never told what it could and could not do with its grants. Under cross-examination by Mike Megaw, she acknowledged that the caucuses did not have to report back to the Legislature on how the grant money was spent, nor were they subject to audits. Ronyk said when a caucus received its grants, people there were expected to follow the honour system to ensure the money was used properly. She says the politicians wanted it that way so they could keep their caucus activities secret from their political opponents.

During his testimony Eric Berntson told the court, "You can fault me for my less than precise record keeping, but you can't fault me for anything improper [and] certainly not criminal." During her testimony, Berntson's wife, Joan, referred to her husband as a "shoe box accountant." She told the court that he still took shoe boxes to his office in the Senate, so receipts and bills wouldn't be scattered everywhere.

The senator also took exception to claims that he had exercised extraordinary power in the Devine government. "I didn't see myself as this powerful dude out there waving a big stick," he said. When asked by his lawyer Mike Megaw whether he had received any cash from John Scraba the senator replied, "He's dead wrong." He said that he and other Conservatives were set up by John Scraba. He related his version of the meeting with Scraba shortly after the police investigation began in the summer of 1991. "He came to my office quite anxious," Berntson testified. Berntson said Scraba told him that if he was going down, he wasn't going down alone. The senator said he arranged for Scraba to get a lawyer and didn't talk to him again.

During cross-examination by Crown prosecutor Sharon Pratchler, it was revealed that Berntson hadn't filed a tax return for his company, Berriedale Management, during the past ten years. The senator said he had tried to file a tax return several years ago with the help of an accountant, but they hadn't been able to find enough records. When asked why he still hadn't filed a return, Berntson replied that it had fallen through the cracks.

Summing up the defence, Mike Megaw suggested that the senator was a victim of poor record-keeping, unscrupulous caucus workers, and an overzealous prosecution. Crown prosecutor Sharon Pratchler described Berntson as a manipulative politician involved in a web of corruption that involved false invoices, numbered companies, and backroom shenanigans. The judge promised a verdict in three weeks, and the senator headed back to his home in Ottawa to wait.

On February 25, 1999, in a packed courtroom, Justice Gerein announced that he found Eric Berntson guilty of making false claims on his Constituency Secretarial and Constituency Office and Services Allowances from 1987 to 1990, stealing nearly $42,000 of taxpayers' money. "I am satisfied beyond a reasonable doubt that the accused devised an illicit scheme whereby he could obtain $41,735," the judge said in his sixty-one-page ruling. The judge acquitted Berntson on the charge of committing a breach of trust involving the $125,000 caucus grant money, and he dismissed the fraud allegations involving Berntson's Communication Allowance.

The fifty-seven-year-old former deputy premier sat motionless as the Queen's Bench justice announced his verdict. He showed no sign of penitence as he left the courthouse. "I am surprised at the verdict," he told the reporters who were waiting for him on the courthouse steps. The usually stony-faced politician appeared to be on the verge of tears. "As far as I'm concerned, I did nothing wrong."

But Justice Gerein obviously saw things differently. He agreed with the Crown that Berntson submitted false invoices on his Constituency Secretarial and Constituency Office and Services Allowances for work that was never done. The judge said the scheme got underway shortly after the Legislature doubled the amount available to MLAs under their Secretarial Allowances. In early 1989, Berntson submitted the first of several claims for "office expenses" incurred by his own company, Berriedale Management Incorporated. The judge found that there was no evidence that Berriedale provided any goods or services on Berntson's behalf. "In short, money flowed from the public purse into his pocket absent any legitimate entitlement. Had the true situation not be concealed by deceit and dishonesty, the money would never have been paid," the judge stated in his ruling.

During the trial, Eric Berntson had argued that he was entitled to the money because it was used to compensate his former wife and current wife for secretarial duties they performed in the home. The judge said he had no doubt that Berntson's ex-wife, Jean Howell, and current wife, Joan Berntson, answered telephone calls, sorted mail, and attended events on Berntson's behalf. But he said they were never paid for their services, nor did they expect to be paid. The judge noted that Berntson continued to bill the Legislature during a seven-month period when he was not living with either woman. "When I consider all the evidence, I am satisfied beyond a reasonable doubt that Berriedale Management Incorporated rendered no services to the accused," he said. "I am likewise satisfied that there was no agreement, arrangement, or even an understanding between the accused and either of his wives that they would be compensated for their labours on his behalf." Justice Gerein touched on the defence argument that other MLAs, including New Democrats and Liberals, had run their constituency offices in a similar fashion. He noted that he didn't know the particulars of those other situations. He said if those situations weren't handled properly, other MLAs might need to be called to account.

Regarding the breach of trust charge involving the $125,000 in grant money that was transferred from the PC caucus to the PC Party, Justice Gerein said he was satisfied that Eric Berntson had asked Lorne McLaren if such a payment was possible, but that he did not order him to do it. And he concluded there was no evidence that direct or indirect coercion was used. He said because Berntson was not responsible for the transfer of the money, there was no need for him to rule on whether the transfer itself was proper. McLaren had pleaded guilty to a similar charge and had served time in jail for it.

Turning to the Crown's allegation that Eric Berntson received $7,870 in kickbacks from John Scraba through his MLA Communication Allowance, the judge said he was not satisfied beyond a reasonable doubt that the senator received the money from the former caucus communications director. He accepted that Berntson asked Scraba to submit expense claims on his behalf, but he wasn't sure if he should believe Scraba when he said he passed the cash on to Berntson in an envelope.

Although he also dismissed allegations of $18,570 in kickbacks involving Berntson's Communication Allowance and Dome Advertising, the judge noted he had some problems with the defence's evidence. Former Dome executive Phil Kershaw testified that he supplied Berntson with a $5,000 invoice for work his company did not perform. When Dome received payment from the Legislature, Kershaw passed the money on to Berriedale at Berntson's request. Berntson said the payments related to a voter-tracking system that Dome wanted to market on his behalf. The judge noted, "I have little confidence in this explanation by the accused, but the explanation could reasonably be true. As a result, I cannot say with certainty why the payments were made by Dome." He said Kershaw's vague and indefinite assertion was also a factor in his decision to dismiss the allegations.

After the guilty verdict on part of the fraud charge raised against him, Berntson formally left his job as deputy opposition leader in the Senate and stopped getting the $9,500 salary top-up that went along with the job. At his sentencing hearing on March 15, 1999, the Crown argued for a prison term, while the defence requested a conditional sentence. Eric Berntson gave an emotional address to the court. His voice cracking at times, he read this prepared statement:

Thank you, my lord. I do have a few words that I would like to say.

First, I would like to thank the court for its wisdom, judgment and fairness throughout these proceedings and deliberations.

Secondly, I want to thank my counsel, Mr. Megaw, for his sage counsel and his quiet effective presence in my defence and for his faith in me throughout.

I was acquitted on a number of counts during these proceedings, for which I am grateful. The one count that I was convicted on will forever form a part of every story that will ever be written or reported on about these matters. That will be my legacy, not my work.

I am the subject of headlines in newsrooms across the country. Judgments about my actions and character have been made against me since these charges were laid and even before these charges were laid.

With the capable advice of my counsel, I resolved to reserve my statements and evidence to proceedings before this court. I maintained that resolve throughout these proceedings out of respect for the judicial process and did not comment to the media during these proceedings.

My counsel has discussed the intense media pressure I have been subjected to. My character has been destroyed. I will have to pay the price for that. My wife and children have also paid a significant price.

My lord may recall coverage with respect to my name

and the Law Society of Saskatchewan. This was a battle I was compelled to fight, even though I have no involvement with that organization, in order that I could defend my name.

Prior to these [proceedings] and law society matters, there were many other proceedings which drained my financial resources and have left a permanent black mark on the Berntson name.

I am now a man of little means. My wife also worked all her life. The money we have earned has gone to pay legal fees and other costs to fight these battles. I was convicted on the charge that dealt with my Constituency and Secretarial Allowance. I was acquitted on all other charges. My lord has noted in his judgment that I was not involved in a communications fund scandal which has plagued this province for the last several years.

I am aware of reports that suggested I was the leader of this scandal. The evidence that I heard at trial confirms that I was not.

While I was pleased and grateful for the acquittals, I am disappointed with the conviction. I have always believed I was acting appropriately and within the rules of the handbook. My lord has judged otherwise. I respect my lord's decision.

I have been proud to serve the people of Saskatchewan, the province of my birth. I have served this province and country in the military, in the Saskatchewan Legislature for 16 years and almost nine years now as a senator.

My service has been with the belief that honesty, integrity and hard work would make a difference for the good of this province. The court's judgment in my case will forever impugn my honesty and integrity. I am hopeful the court will allow me to continue my work. I have dedicated a great deal of my time to community issues. Caring for those less fortunate, respecting that all people—no matter what station in life—have certain fundamental rights.

Children and youth issues are very close to my heart. I used my time to further those issues through advocacy, awareness building, fundraising—be it Big Brothers, the United Way, Saskatchewan Science Centre, the Learning

Disabilities Association of Saskatchewan. I remain commit-
ted to these causes. This is my life's work. There is no rec-
ompense for this work, but the feeling of satisfaction I hold
inside knowing that I have been part of the process of get-
ting one more street kid reunited with his family—that is
payment enough, my lord.

I say this not for my recognition. My role has been that
of a quiet advocate, working to make society a better place.
A better place for our youth, our future.

I say this, my lord, so that you may have some insight
as to who I really am. I ask for you to balance my positive
contributions to our society with those which you have found
me guilty.

There is no one to blame but myself. I accept full respon-
sibility for my shortcomings. Ignorance is no defence. For
my indiscretions, I am profoundly sorry.

I attempted to convey during the trial that the dealings
with these allowances were my dealings alone and it is I who
must accept the blame. I must respect your decision and I do.

A finding of guilty on this charge will result in resign-
ing my seat in the Senate, 23 years short of its natural
course—not an insignificant penalty, my lord.

I apologize to the court and to the people I have served.
I apologize to my family. It is all quite sad for them.

After 30 years of serving my country and my province
with hard work and dedication, this conviction forever will
be on the Berntson name. Again, my lord, I apologize.

Berntson's lawyer, Mike Megaw, told the judge that the former deputy premier would resign his seat in the Senate if his
conviction was upheld on appeal. Megaw argued for a conditional sentence, which would allow the senator to return to his
home in Ottawa and serve his sentence in the community.
Megaw noted that conditional sentences are available to those
convicted of fraud involving less than $100,000. He pointed out
that former Tory MLA Harry Baker and caucus employee
Michael McCafferty had both received conditional sentences for
offences involving from $22,000 to $36,000.

Crown prosecutor Sharon Pratchler turned to the well-known musical Les Misérables and its tragic hero for some of her arguments. "This is no Jean Val Jean before the court," she said. "He did not have to defraud the public in order to put a loaf of bread on the table." She argued that Saskatchewan courts have consistently sentenced those convicted of fraud of more than $20,000 to a period of incarceration, unless there were unusual circumstances. "If the public cannot trust those who make the law, then who can they trust?" she asked. It was an argument she had used at previous sentencing hearings for convicted Tories. She argued that if Berntson had been experiencing financial difficulties when the crimes were committed, he had other options, such as curtailing his lifestyle.

Pratchler asked the Court of Queen's Bench justice to send Eric Berntson to jail for a term of eighteen to twenty-four months. The judge said he would hand down his sentence the next day. Senator Eric Berntson and his wife, Joan, held hands as they walked out of the courthouse and past the horde of reporters and cameras waiting for them. As usual, the senator looked straight ahead and ignored the barrage of questions thrown his way by journalists.

The next day, before he handed down the sentence, Justice Gerein noted that it "should be made known to others that dishonesty in public office will result in harsh sentences." Speaking directly to Berntson, he said, "Over the years, you have done much good; however, the fact remains you did steal almost $42,000. It was not the result of deprivation. It was motivated by greed and committed while you were in high office." He went on to say, "It's also a sad day for the whole of society. When a leader does wrong, all its citizens feel a sense of disappointment. They lose confidence in government. Cynicism sets in and that is harmful to the entire social fabric." The judge concluded, "I consider your offence to be serious and the sentence must reflect that."

Justice Gerein rejected Eric Berntson's plea for leniency and sentenced him to a year in jail and ordered him to pay restitution of $41,735, the same amount he illegally received from his constituency office expense allowances. Joan Berntson, who by this time was reduced to tears, embraced her husband before he was escorted from the courtroom in handcuffs. His lawyer, Mike Megaw, immediately filed an appeal with the Saskatchewan Court of Appeal, and four hours later the senator and his wife were on a plane heading back to Ottawa.

In Ottawa, MPs with the Reform and New Democratic parties started clamouring for Berntson's resignation. They argued that if he wasn't prepared to step down, he should at least give up his salary until all appeals were exhausted. Senators earn $64,500 a year in salary, an additional $10,000 in tax-free expense allowance, plus a $9,000 housing allowance. Berntson kept his seat in the Senate and continued to attend sessions regularly.

The Constitution Act, 1867, states that any senator convicted of a felony or infamous crime must vacate his or her seat. The problem is that the term felony was eliminated from the Criminal Code more than a hundred years ago. It's now up to the Senate to decide how to proceed if a senator is convicted and won't resign. The Senate has never determined what constitutes an "infamous" crime. Gordon Barnhard, a former clerk of the Senate, explained, "On any case where senators are in this circumstance and the appeal process is exhausted, then the Senate will entertain a motion that a seat be declared vacant. There would be a debate and ultimately, a vote." He noted that has never happened. The rules say a senator who is kicked out loses his or her pension but is entitled to receive his or her own pension contributions. If the senator quits first, as Eric Berntson vowed to do if he lost his appeal, he or she keeps the pension.

While Eric Berntson waited for his appeal to be heard, there was more fallout from his trial. At the sentencing hearing, Mike Megaw had produced a stack of letters of support for his client for the judge's consideration. Eric Berntson received letters of reference from a number of prominent people inside and outside Saskatchewan. They included a lawyer, a minister, and other senators. One of the letters came from Saskatoon Police Chief Dave Scott. Scott wrote the one-page letter, dated March 3 and typed on Saskatoon Police Service letterhead, at Megaw's request.

In the letter, which was written one week after Berntson was convicted, Scott related how he met Berntson in 1992 when he was working on an experimental community police station in Saskatoon. He wrote that Berntson and his wife, Joan, helped obtain a computer program for the station through the Saskatchewan Literacy Foundation. When the letter became public, some members of the board of the police commission in Saskatoon weren't pleased. The mayor said it was unfortunate that the letter was written on official police letterhead. Another member questioned whether it was appropriate for the chief of police or any police officer to send letters of reference or support for convicted criminals.

"My comments were just a matter of fact as to what he had provided me as a sergeant in implementing the experimental police station," Scott replied. "Any letter I would send, I would send on police letterhead. It was a police matter in relation to a police program. I don't think it would have mattered if it was on plain paper. What people are looking at is who signed it." It was a flash in the pan, and the issue died within days.

On April 28, 2000, the Saskatchewan Court of Appeal, in a two-to-one split decision, upheld Berntson's conviction and sentence. Justices Cal Tallis and Nicholas Sherstobitoff were in concurrence with the trial judge; Justice William Vancise dissented. The door was open for an automatic appeal to the Supreme Court of Canada.

In their majority decision, the two justices wrote, "We observe that a heavy trust and responsibility is placed in the hands of those holding public office or employ. The public are entitled to expect persons in such positions to observe the 'honour' system that they have put in place when it comes to the expenditures of public funds for various allowances."

In his dissenting opinion, Justice William Vancise wrote that the Crown had failed to prove beyond a reasonable doubt that Berntson set out to commit fraud. "What was relevant, but not determined by the trial judge," he wrote, "was whether Mr. Berntson believed he was entitled to the funds." Justice Vancise went on to say that in the circumstances of this case, "I would exercise my discretion and direct that a verdict of acquittal be submitted for the conviction rather than order a new trial." The justice didn't end his comments there. He went on to say that given the decision of the majority on the conviction appeal and sentence appeal, it was necessary for him to consider the appropriateness of the sentence. He concluded that he would set aside the custodial sentence of one year to be served in prison and impose a conditional sentence of imprisonment of fifteen months to be served in the community under house arrest or even electronic monitoring.

The senator was in Ottawa when the appeal court decision was released. His lawyer immediately began making arrangements for a bail hearing while he prepared the documents for an appeal to the Supreme Court of Canada. Four days later, Eric Berntson flew to Regina and early the following morning, as arranged by his lawyer, turned himself in to police. He was held in custody in a jail cell until early afternoon, then he was brought to the courthouse in handcuffs for his bail hearing. The hearing took about fifteen minutes. The handcuffs were removed and the senator walked out of the courthouse, past the media, and into a waiting van. Berntson returned to Ottawa and his duties as a senator. The calls for his resignation resumed, but Berntson stubbornly clung to his seat in the Senate hoping for the best when the Supreme Court heard his appeal. At the time of writing, that appeal is pending.

Twelve former Tory MLAs and two caucus employees had now been convicted as a result of Project Fiddle. Four MLAs had been acquitted. The charges against a special advisor to the premier had been dismissed. The case of one other former MLA, Ralph Katzman, was still before the court.

The Tory Casket

Throughout the 1990s, the fraud scandal hung over the heads of the Saskatchewan Tories like a heavy cloud. The New Conservatives, under the leadership of Bill Boyd, tried to distance themselves from the trials, and the New Democrats were poised to run up the torn and tattered Tory fraud flag whenever they felt the political right breathing down their necks. The big question—how could this happen?—hung in the air.

Even though he was the official head of the Conservative government during the fraud years, Grant Devine was never tied to the scandal in any significant way. People tried, especially some of those who were convicted, and there was lots of whispering. The RCMP, however, didn't uncover any evidence that indicated that the former premier had broken the law or even knew about the fraud scheme operating in his caucus office.

"I feel betrayed like a lot of others feel," Devine said during an interview with a reporter in April 1995. "We trusted individuals." He said he was saddened by the turn of events and wondered what had set it all off. "The questions that keep coming up are Why pick on these people?" he asked. "And why now? And how long has this strategy to embarrass these people been going on?" He pointed out how the investigation had severely disrupted the lives of many it had touched. "It is a political reality that politics is in good part based on innuendo, not . . . on the facts. So people want to use this against individuals. . . . The consequences for people's lives [are] devastating and for some your whole role in politics is not only your self-image, but your community image. All of these people are good solid citizens."

Devine said that a premier can't be blamed for the conduct of the people around him. "How much did the kickbacks that

Phoenix gave an NDP cabinet minister [Murray Koskie] have to do with Roy Romanow? How much? Was he part of it? Did he know about it?" He said what concerned him most was the motive behind the police investigation. "You got to ask who is in charge of it?" he said. "Who talks about it? Who runs the Legislative Assembly? Who is in government?"

After the New Democrats' win in the 1991 provincial election, Grant Devine continued to sit as the MLA for Estevan. He retired as leader of the Conservative Party the following year. At his November 1992 retirement party in Saskatoon, the Conservative Party gave him a saddle, a shotgun, and a rifle as going-away presents. He went back to teaching agriculture part-time at the University of Saskatchewan and didn't run in the 1995 provincial election. He set up a Regina consulting company called Grant Devine Management Inc. He continued to operate the family's large farm holdings near Moose Jaw, and he continued to dabble in politics behind the scenes.

Badly bruised because of Project Fiddle, the Saskatchewan Tory Party has struggled to stay alive. According to some political observers, no other government or political party in Canada has been so thoroughly and publicly discredited. In preparing for the 1995 provincial election, Conservative Leader Bill Boyd tried to distance his Tories from the past by changing the party's name to the New PCs. During the election campaign, some candidates went so far as to leave their party affiliation off their lawn signs, but it didn't help. The Tories won only five seats with just under 18 percent of the vote. All five seats were rural, four of them in loyal Conservative constituencies. Boyd continued to try to convince people that the fraud scandal was not the "failing of a philosophy or a party" but the "failings of people within."

According to political pundits, it was partly the arrogance of the people within that brought the Saskatchewan Tory Party to its knees. The caucus ship was loose on the high political seas with no rudder, while the crew in the caucus galley were fighting over the scraps of power. For some, the prize was a few dollars to pay for saddles, baseball hats, and trinkets to hand out in coffee shops to buy votes. For others, the prize was padding their expense accounts with their personal allowances. For yet others, like Lorne McLaren and John Scraba, the prize was pooling money to do battle with the socialists in the media. Somewhere along the way, the pooling system got caught in the current with no one to steer it out to calmer waters.

David Smith, a professor of political science at the University of Saskatchewan, thinks this lack of direction may have had its roots in the Tories stunning 1982 victory over the NDP. The Tories swept in on a tidal wave of power and most of those elected had never been in political life before. There were few older members they could look to for guidance in their new roles, and some members may have gotten carried away in their inexperience. The end result, he says, was a one gigantic scandal unparalleled anywhere else in Canada.

The scandal dogged the lives of many of the old-guard Tories. Rick Swenson, who took over the reins of the party for a while after Grant Devine stepped aside, explained what it was like trying to shake off the disgrace. In a statement issued in 1997, shortly after six of his former colleagues had been charged, Swenson said that he and his family had to live with people's reactions every day. "I am a member of that former government and as such cannot go to church on Sunday," he told reporters at a news conference in a Regina hotel. "I can't go to watch my sons' school basketball games. I went to a friend's child's funeral a week and a half ago and I [got] asked the question all the time, 'Are you next?'" He said as long as the police investigation was ongoing, the cloud of suspicion hung over his head and over the heads of many others.

Like many others, Swenson questioned why the investigation took so long. Some Tories lived under a cloud of suspicion for six years before they were charged. Neither the RCMP nor the Crown prosecutor's office responded to these criticisms. The province's executive director of public prosecution, Richard Quinney, did, however, comment that it took a long time to map the paper trail through the thousands of financial documents seized in Project Fiddle as there was a shortage of the highly trained forensic investigators to tackle complicated fraud cases.

Swenson and other Tories also wondered why many of the

cases that involved the Communication Allowances weren't dealt with internally at the Legislature, instead of coming before the courts. There had been other cases in which MLAs had received payments from allowances that should not have been approved. In those instances, the MLAs were required to repay the money, without any criminal charges being laid. The RCMP were made aware of the allegations that the NDP were doing the same thing as the Tories with their allowances, but they had no reason to investigate because no official complaint was filed.

The rules of accountability for caucuses have changed dramatically since Project Fiddle unearthed the corruption in the PC caucus office. The chances of anyone personally handling thousands of dollars in caucus funds for any party are now slim. Prior to Project Fiddle, caucuses were expected to follow the honour system to ensure the money was spent for its intended purposes: research, secretarial, and other general expenses. In practice, politicians often viewed caucus money as a war chest to help fight the next provincial election, and records were destroyed at the end of each year. That way, the caucuses could keep their activities secret from their political opponents and the media.

That all changed in the mid-1990s. In 1993, caucuses were required to provide a letter stating that the books had been audited, but there were no details on the findings and no requirement that the information be made public. In 1994, the NDP cabinet established an independent committee on MLA compensation to make recommendations on salaries, allowances, and reimbursement of expenses. As a result of the committee's work, which included public hearings, the all-party Board of Internal Economy established new rules and procedures for all expenses, including the caucus accounts.

All caucus offices are now required to submit audited financial statements and audited schedules of capital assets each year. The reports are available for public viewing and are tabled in the Legislature. The provincial auditor, however, thinks the Board of Internal Economy needs to further improve its rules and procedures to ensure that caucus offices manage public money appropriately. Among other things, he recommended that the Legislative Assembly be provided with a list of persons who receive public money from caucus offices, including the amounts received.

Another fallout from Project Fiddle was an examination of the justice system. There were questions about some of the decisions coming out of the courts in the fraud cases. Clyne Harradence, the lawyer closest to the Tory fraud scandal, pointed out that there were many similarities in the charges laid against the twenty Tories nabbed in Project Fiddle. Much of the evidence submitted during each court case was similar and was provided by many of the same witnesses. Yet the outcomes in the cases were often quite different. Some of Harradence's clients were exonerated, while others were convicted. After one of his clients, Harold Martens, was found guilty of fraud, Harradence questioned whether the system was working properly. "It's impossible. Four different judges dealing with almost identical facts and witnesses," he said. "It's the system [that] ain't working very well if it just depends on the judge. But that's the way the process works," he added. "And you know, it's the impressions that the individual judge gets in the interpretation of the evidence and that's why there is this difference."

Then there is the question of the punishment handed out to those found guilty. Even though the Crown pushed for jail sentences for Tories that either pleaded guilty or were convicted, only five—Lorne McLaren, John Scraba, Michael Hopfner, John Gerich, and Eric Berntson—were actually put behind bars. Berntson, who has appealed to the Supreme Court of Canada, was detained for only a few hours. One provincial court judge, when considering a proper sentence during a guilty plea, questioned the Crown on why it had not appealed any of the conditional discharges and fines that had been handed to other convicted Tories. (With a conditional discharge there is no criminal record once the person has completed the conditions imposed, such as probation and community service work.) Eric Neufeld, the Crown prosecutor in the case, replied that the decision on whether to appeal was made by people higher up in the

Justice Department. The judge noted that welfare recipients have gone to jail for defrauding the government, and farmers have gone to jail for defrauding crop insurance. He expressed the view that the convicted Tory who was before him (Joan Duncan) should be given a jail term, but his hands were tied because of the precedents established by previous sentencing of Tories convicted in Project Fiddle.

Similar issues were discussed in another case where a convicted Tory was sent to jail. Before handing down a sentence to Michael Hopfner, the justice of the Court of Queen's Bench explained why he felt a lengthy term of incarceration was necessary. "When it comes to the crime of fraud, single mothers who, out of desperation, cheat on welfare, have most often gone to jail," the justice said. "Impoverished family breadwinners, who, also out of desperation, cheat on unemployment insurance, have most often gone to jail." He went on to say that some others "who have illegally obtained money from the government of Saskatchewan by means of false expense claims, have gone to jail, though not all." In this case, Michael Hopfner was sentenced to eighteen months behind bars.

In yet another case, a judge determined that former cabinet minister Sherwin Petersen was "duped." Even though he found him guilty of fraud involving just over $9,000, Petersen was given a conditional discharge, with probation, community service work, and a restitution order. The Crown appealed, but lost.

John Gerich was the only Tory to put his faith in the hands of a jury. When all the evidence was in (evidence quite similar to that submitted at other fraud trials), the jury found the former cabinet minister guilty of helping to organize and operate the fraud scheme in the PC caucus office. They also found him guilty of illegally receiving just over $12,000 in cash and equipment. Gerich was sentenced to two years less a day.

In another case, the judge commented that "our sentences in this area used to be relatively clear. They aren't very clear anymore." Some people think that the different conclusions reached by different judges weighing similar evidence in Project Fiddle has eroded the public's confidence in the justice system, especially when it comes to sentencing.

A number of the Tories convicted of fraud still maintain their innocence. Some may have been caught up in the fraud scheme because of their inexperience and their trust in those they believed knew how things worked, but others, like Lorne McLaren and John Scraba, were too deeply involved with secret caucus companies, safety deposit boxes filled with $1,000 bills, and false expense claims not to realize they were bending the rules at best. Grant Schmidt, a former Tory cabinet minister and a lawyer, pointed out that many good, honest people were victims of what happened in the caucus office. "If you're an honest politician doing an honest job," he said, "you get tainted by the dishonest." Schmidt said he had no idea what was going on in the caucus office. "You expect the caucus chair to do his job," he said. At the time he was interviewed, after testifying at Michael Hopfner's trial in September of 1996, Schmidt felt the Tory Party would recover from Project Fiddle. Others, inside and outside the party, weren't as confident and began looking for another road back to power.

In 1997, the Saskatchewan Liberal Party, the official opposition in the Legislature, was struggling with internal bickering. Its new leader, Jim Melenchuk was having trouble keeping his caucus in line. Melenchuk didn't have a seat in the Legislature. He had replaced Lynda Haverstock, who had been ousted in a bitter leadership feud in 1995. On August 8, 1997, four disgruntled Liberal MLAs quit their party and joined four Conservatives to form the Saskatchewan Party. The new party was a coalition of Liberal, Conservative, and federal Reform Party members. Its leader was Saskatchewan farmer and former federal Reform MP Elwin Hermanson. The other sitting Conservative MLA at the time, Jack Goohsen, was not invited into the Saskatchewan Party fold. Goohsen, a fifty-six-year-old, cowboy-hat-totin' farmer from the province's southwest had been charged after he was caught with a fourteen-year-old prostitute that spring. The last thing the Saskatchewan Party wanted was a tainted Tory in its ranks. Two years after he was caught with the prostitute, Gooshen was convicted of buying sex from a teenager and was given a four-month conditional sentence to be served in the community. Facing a threat of being suspended without pay while any appeals were going through the courts, Goohsen resigned his seat in the Legislature. His appeal to the Saskatchewan Court of Appeal was dismissed, as was his appeal to the Supreme Court of Canada.

On August 21, 1997, the Saskatchewan Party, with eight members, replaced the Liberals as the official opposition. There were three independents at the time: former Liberal leader Lynda Haverstock, former Liberal Arlene Jule, and Jack Goohsen. The Liberals described the new Saskatchewan Party as "nothing more than the old Tories with a new coat of paint to hide the rust and the rot underneath." The New Democrats continued to call them the Tories.

On November 9, 1997, the Saskatchewan Conservative Party was laid to rest with no guarantee it would ever be brought back to life. Delegates at a convention voted 130 to 32 to render the party "inactive" for the next two provincial elections, a period of five to seven years. The delegates chose ten trustees and gave them the power to decide whether the party should be revived at the end of the hiatus. The trustees would have to run ten candidates in each of the next two provincial elections in order to keep their status as a registered political party. The candidates would be handpicked. They wouldn't spend any money nor would they do any campaigning. They would just be paper candidates who wouldn't actually be looking for votes. As one supporter of the Saskatchewan Party put it, "the Conservative Party certainly isn't dead, it's just keeping its head low." The Tory fraud scandal had brought the Provincial Conservative Party to the brink of extinction, a ninety-year history put on hold because of Project Fiddle.

It wasn't long before the Saskatchewan Party tried some mud-slinging of its own, a smear campaign against the New Democrats with members' allowances at the centre—some of the same allowances that had gotten a lot of Tories in trouble with the law. During the 1999 session of the Legislature, the Saskatchewan Party accused some New Democrats of misusing taxpayers' money, alleging that in some cases, the use of the money may have been illegal. The Saskatchewan Party asked the RCMP to look into how ten NDP members ran their constituency offices in the 1980s and early 1990s. All of the members had set up non-profit corporations to run their offices, and in some cases the corporations had money left over when all the bills were paid. In one instance, about $11,000 was used to set up a scholarship fund to honour former premier Allan Blakeney.

The Saskatchewan Party filed a complaint with the RCMP on March 26. In early June, the RCMP stated in a letter to the Saskatchewan Party that they found no grounds for a criminal investigation. Responding to the police decision, former Tory leader and now Saskatchewan Party member Bill Boyd said, "We are certainly disappointed. We think there were many parallels between the actions of New Democrats and [Senator Eric] Berntson's case. It appeared to us that they were very, very similar in nature." The Saskatchewan Party refused to release the letter it received from the RCMP. Boyd said, "We just don't feel it's appropriate to release communication between the RCMP and ourselves." A columnist with the Regina *Leader-Post* described the Saskatchewan Party complaint as "pure and simple pre-election mud-slinging."

The headline in the Friday, September 17, 1999, *Leader-Post*, the day after the provincial election, read "Razor-Thin Win." The New Democrats, with Roy Romanow at the helm, took twenty-nine seats with 38.7 percent of the popular vote. The Saskatchewan Party, led by Elwin Hermanson, took twenty-six seats with 39.6 percent of the popular vote, just shy of a percentage point higher than the NDP, while the Liberals took three seats with 20.2 percent of the popular vote. The Saskatchewan Party captured most of the seats in rural areas, a traditional Conservative stronghold, while the NDP held on because of its traditional support in the cities. The New Democrats' attempts throughout the campaign to tie the Saskatchewan Party with the scandal-plagued Tories (its so-called Sask-a-Tory campaign) obviously didn't work or at least wasn't a factor in the minds of many voters. Soon after the election, the New Democrats and the Liberals joined forces to form a coalition government.

In the year 2000, after nearly a decade of capturing headlines, the Tory fraud scandal appears to be taking a back seat to more immediate political issues, such as tax cuts and health care. As one small-town newspaper editor commented to a reporter, "I don't think anyone cares anymore. There's been so much of it." The voters seem to have put the affair behind them, turning out in good numbers for the 1999 provincial election and showing strong support for the Saskatchewan Party, even knowing many of its members are former Tories. As for the legacy of the Grant Devine government, political scientist David Smith, who has studied prairie politics for thirty-five years, doesn't think people will refer to the Tory government of the 1980s without in the next breath mentioning the scandals. "Whatever else the government did," he said, "Those scandals put all else into shadows."

Appendix

Summary of Cases in Project Fiddle

The following summary is arranged in chronological order according to the date each case came to trial or a plea was entered. It covers only those cases of Conservatives connected with Project Fiddle.

✤ ✤ ✤

Name: Lorne McLaren

Position(s) held: MLA for Yorkton, cabinet minister, caucus chair.

Charge: Charged late June 1994 with two counts of fraud over $1,000, one count of conspiracy to commit fraud over $1,000, one count of theft over $1,000, and two counts of breach of trust. Accused of submitting false expense claims to get $33,000 from his MLA Communication Allowance; stealing $114,200 from the PC caucus account; diverting $125,000 from the PC caucus fund to the PC Party of Saskatchewan; and conspiring with John Scraba to commit fraud and with defrauding taxpayers of $837,000.

Preliminary hearing: Commenced on November 7, 1994.

Trial: Commenced on May 15, 1995, Court of Queen's Bench Justice Isadore Grotsky presiding; Crown prosecutor, Eric Neufeld; defence lawyer, Neil Halford, replaced by David Birchard.

Pleaded guilty: Pleaded guilty on June 27, 1995, to three

charges (fraud charge involving over $837,000 in public money, breach of trust in connection with the diversion of $125,000 from the PC caucus account to the PC Party of Saskatchewan, and charge of stealing $114,200); the other three charges (conspiracy to defraud, breach of trust by a public official in connection with stealing $114,200, and fraud by a public official) were stayed.

Sentence: Sentenced on November 12, 1995, to three and a half years in prison for fraud, two and a half years for theft, and two and a half years for diverting funds, terms to be served concurrently.

✢ ✢ ✢

Name: John Scraba

Position(s) held: Communications director, PC caucus office.

Charge: Charged in July 1994 with one count of fraud over $1,000, one count of conspiracy to commit fraud, and possession of the proceeds of fraud, relating to $240,000 cash and a vehicle.

Preliminary hearing: December 5, 1994.

Pleaded guilty: Pleaded guilty on November 8, 1995, to a charge of defrauding the Government of Saskatchewan of $837,000. In return, the other charges were stayed. Court of Queen's Bench Justice Ted Noble presiding; Crown prosecutor, Eric Neufeld; defence lawyer, Bill McIsaac.

Sentence: Sentenced on November 8, 1995, to two years less a day and ordered to pay restitution of $12,000.

✢ ✢ ✢

Name: Lorne Kopelchuk

Position(s) held: MLA for Canora and cabinet minister.

Charge: Charged in April 1995 with one count of fraud under $5,000. Accused of submitting a false expense claim for "Audio presentation: speeches, materials" to get $1,568 from his Communication Allowance to purchase a portable, electronic public address system.

Trial: Commenced on September 18, 1995, Provincial Court Judge Janet McMurtry presiding; Crown prosecutor, Eric Neufeld; defence lawyer, Orest Rosowsky.

Acquitted: September 28, 1995.

✢ ✢ ✢

Name: Grant Hodgins

Position(s) held: MLA for Melfort and cabinet minister.

Charge: Charged in April 1995 with one count of fraud under $5,000. Accused of using a false expense claim for "Audio presentation: speeches" to get $3,645 from his Communication Allowance to purchase computer software.

Trial: Commenced on October 31, 1995, Provincial Court Judge Diane Morris presiding; Crown prosecutor, Eric Neufeld; defence lawyer, Stuart Eisner.

Verdict: Found guilty on December 15, 1995.

Sentence: Sentenced on January 19, 1996. Granted a conditional discharge. Ordered to pay restitution of $3,645 and to perform 240 hours of community service work.

✢ ✢ ✢

Name: John Britton

Position(s) held: MLA for Wilkie.

Charge: Charged in April 1995 with two counts of fraud under $5,000. Accused of submitting a false expense claim for "Audio/video Presentation: materials, speeches" to get $3,500 from his Communication Allowance; and of submitting a false expense claim for "Newsletters: Constituents of Wilkie" to get $2,300 from his Communication Allowance to purchase a video camera.

Trial: Commenced on November 27, 1995, Provincial Court Judge Bruce Henning presiding; Crown prosecutor, Eric Neufeld; defence lawyer, Clyne Harradence.

Acquitted: November 30, 1995.

❖ ❖ ❖

Name: William Neudorf

Position(s) held: MLA for Rosthern and cabinet minister.

Charge: Charged in April 1995 with one count of fraud under $5,000. Accused of submitting a false expense claim for "Newsletter: constituents of Rosthern" to get $1,050 from his Communication Allowance.

Trial: Commenced on December 4, 1995, Provincial Court Judge Harvie Allan presiding; Crown prosecutor, Eric Neufeld; defence lawyer Clyne Harradence.

Acquitted: January 15, 1996.

❖ ❖ ❖

Name: Harold Martens

Position(s) held: MLA for Morse and cabinet minister.

Charge: Charged April 1995 with two counts of fraud under $5,000. Accused of submitting two false expense claims for "Newsletters: Constituents of Morse and for photo distribution" to get $3,600 from his Communication Allowance to purchase a computer; and of submitting a false expense claim for "Video presentations: consultation; materials" to get $2,250 from his Communication Allowance to purchase a video camera.

Trial: Commenced on December 11, 1995, Provincial Court Judge Leslie Halliday presiding; Crown prosecutor, Eric Neufeld; defence lawyer, Clyne Harradence.

Verdict: Found guilty on February 15, 1996.

Sentence: Sentenced on April 10, 1996. Granted a conditional discharge. Ordered to pay restitution of $5,850 and to perform 240 hours of community service work.

✢ ✢ ✢

Name: Ray Meiklejohn

Position(s) held: MLA for Saskatoon-River Heights and cabinet minister.

Charge: Charged April 1995 with one count of fraud under $5,000. Accused of submitting a false expense claim for "newsletters" to get $4,520 from his Communication Allowance to purchase a computer.

Trial: Commenced on December 18, 1995, Provincial Court Judge Ross Moxley presiding; Crown prosecutor, Eric Neufeld; defence lawyer, Orest Rosowsky.

Verdict: Found guilty on January 25, 1996.

Sentence: Granted a conditional discharge. Ordered to pay restitution of $4,500 and to perform 240 hours of community service. Placed on probation for a year.

Appeal: Appeal before the Saskatchewan Court of Appeal rejected December 1996.

✣ ✣ ✣

Name: Joan Duncan

Position(s) held: MLA for Maple Creek and cabinet minister.

Charge: Charged April 1995 with one count of fraud over $5,000. Accused of submitting false expense claims to get $12,405 from her Communication Allowance.

Preliminary hearing: Commenced on November 15, 1995.

Pleaded guilty: Pleaded guilty on April 11, 1996, Provincial Court Judge Ken Bellerose presiding; Crown prosecutor, Eric Neufeld; defence lawyer, Fred Kovach.

Sentence: Sentenced on May 28, 1996. Fined $5,000, ordered to pay restitution of $12,405, and placed on probation for a year.

✣ ✣ ✣

Name: Michael Hopfner

Position(s) held: MLA for Cut Knife–Lloydminster and caucus whip.

Charge: Charged in April 1995 with two counts of fraud over $5,000 and one count of conspiracy to commit fraud over $5,000. Accused of submitting false expense claims to get $57,348 from his Communication Allowance, and of conspiring with John Scraba to commit fraud and with defrauding taxpayers of $837,000.

Preliminary hearing: Commenced on January 29, 1996.

Trial: Commenced on September 3, 1996, Court of Queen's Bench Justice Ross Wimmer presiding; Crown prosecutor, Eric Neufeld; Hopfner defended himself.

Verdict: Found guilty on November 15, 1996, of receiving $57,348 after making false claims on his Communication Allowance; not guilty of one charge of fraud and one charge of conspiracy.

Sentence: Sentenced on January 6, 1997, to eighteen months in jail and ordered to pay restitution of $56,000.

✤ ✤ ✤

Name: John Gerich

Position(s) held: MLA for Redberry, caucus whip, cabinet minister.

Charge: Charged in April 1995 with two counts of fraud over $5,000 and one count of conspiracy to commit fraud over $5,000. Accused of submitting false expense claims to get cash, a computer hard drive, and a portable electronic public address system worth a total of $12,264 through his Communication Allowance. Also accused of conspiring with John Scraba to commit fraud and with defrauding taxpayers of $837,000.

Preliminary hearing: November 27, 1995.

Trial: Elected to be tried by judge and jury. Trial commenced on January 20, 1997, Court of Queen's Bench Justice William Matheson presiding; Crown prosecutor, Sharon Pratchler; Gerich defended himself.

Verdict: Found guilty on February 6, 1997, on two charges of fraud; cleared of conspiracy to commit fraud.

Sentence: Sentenced on February 21, 1997, to two years less a day and ordered to pay restitution of $12,264.

✤ ✤ ✤

Name: Robert Andrew

Position(s) held: MLA for Kindersley and cabinet minister.

Charge: Charged in January 1997 with one count of fraud under $5,000. Accused of submitting a false expense claim for advertising to get approximately $4,500 from his Communication Allowance to pay his constituency secretary.

Pleaded guilty: Pleaded guilty on May 8, 1997, Provincial Court Judge Diane Morris presiding; Crown prosecutor, Sharon Pratchler; defence lawyer, Gordon Kuski.

Sentence: Sentenced on May 23, 1997. Fined $5,000 and ordered to pay restitution of $4,224.27.

✢ ✢ ✢

Name: Sherwin Petersen

Position(s) held: MLA for Kelvington-Wadena and cabinet minister.

Charge: Charged in April 1995, on two counts of fraud over $5,000 and one count of conspiracy to commit fraud over $5,000. Accused of submitting false expense claims to get $9,285 from his Communication Allowance to purchase a video camera, a computer, and a computer hard drive, and of conspiring with John Scraba to commit fraud and with defrauding taxpayers of $837,000.

Preliminary hearing: January 1996.

Trial: Commenced on February 10, 1997; delayed until May 20, 1997, Court of Queen's Bench Justice Omer Archambault presiding; Crown prosecutor, Sharon Pratchler; defence lawyers Clyne Harradence (lead lawyer) and Kevin Mellor (lawyer and chartered accountant).

Verdict: Found guilty on July 15 of one count of fraud over $5,000; acquitted on second charge of fraud and of charge of conspiracy with John Scraba to commit fraud.

Sentence: Sentenced on August 25, 1997. Granted a conditional discharge, placed on probation for three years, ordered to perform 240 hours of community service work, and ordered to pay restitution of $9,285.

✣ ✣ ✣

Name: Harry Baker

Position(s) held: MLA for Biggar, PC whip, and PC caucus chair.

Charge: Charged in April 1995 with one count of fraud over $5,000. Accused of submitting false expense claims to get $22,545 from his Communication Allowance.

Preliminary hearing: Commenced on February 26, 1996.

Trial: Commenced on November 12, 1997, Court of Queen's Bench Justice Eugene Scheibel presiding; Crown prosecutor, Sharon Pratchler; defence lawyer, Rod Donlevy.

Verdict: Found guilty on February 19, 1998.

Sentence: Sentenced on April 17, 1998. Given a one-year conditional sentence with a curfew restricting his movement to his farm east of Saskatoon for the first four months; ordered to pay restitution of $22,545.

✣ ✣ ✣

Name: Michael McCafferty

Position(s) held: PC caucus researcher and speechwriter.

Charge: Charged in January 1997 with one count of fraud over $5,000. Accused of submitting false expense claims to get $36,657 from his Communication Allowance.

Pleaded guilty: Pleaded guilty on October 6, 1997, Provincial

Court Judge Dennis Fenwick presiding; Crown prosecutor, Sharon Pratchler; defence lawyer, Robert Skinner.

Sentence: Sentenced on December 16, 1997, to one year to be served in the community and ordered to perform sixty hours of community service.

✤ ✤ ✤

Name: Donald Pringle

Position(s) held: Special advisor to Grant Devine and executive director of the PC Party of Saskatchewan.

Charge: Charged in January 1997 with one count of fraud over $5,000 in connection with the $125,000 transferred from the PC caucus account to the PC Party of Saskatchewan in 1987.

Preliminary hearing: Commenced on October 20, 1997; Provincial Court Judge Bruce Henning presiding; Crown prosecutor, Sharon Pratchler assisted by Brent Klaus; defence lawyer, Michael Megaw.

Charges dismissed: December 18, 1997.

✤ ✤ ✤

Name: Robert Pickering

Position(s) held: MLA for Bengough-Milestone and cabinet minister.

Charge: Charged in January 1997 with one count of fraud over $5,000. Accused of submitting false expense claims to get $27,000 from his Communication Allowance.

Trial: Commenced on May 4, 1998, Provincial Court Judge Dennis Fenwick presiding; Crown prosecutor, Sharon Pratchler; defence lawyer, Gordon Kuski.

Acquitted: May 26, 1998.

✣ ✣ ✣

Name: Senator Eric Berntson

Position(s) held: MLA for Souris-Cannington and deputy premier.

Charge: Charged in January 1997 with two counts of fraud over $5,000 and one count of breach of trust. Accused of defrauding the public of $68,055 using three different methods on three different expense allowances and of allegedly assisting in the diversion of $125,000 from the PC caucus account to the PC Party of Saskatchewan early in 1987.

Preliminary hearing: Commenced on October 20, 1997, Provincial Court Judge Bruce Henning presiding; Crown prosecutor, Sharon Pratchler; defence lawyer, Clyne Harradence. Berntson agreed to go to trial on one of the fraud charges a few hours before the preliminary hearing concluded. On January 19, 1998, Judge Henning dismissed the fraud charge involving the $125,000, but ordered the senator to stand trial on the breach of trust charge involving the same money.

Trial: Commenced on January 11, 1999, Court of Queen's Bench Justice Frank Gerein presiding; Crown prosecutor, Sharon Pratchler assisted by Brent Klaus; defence lawyer, Mike Megaw.

Verdict: Found guilty on February 25, 1999, of part of the fraud charge, but acquitted on charge of breach of trust.

Sentence: Sentenced on March 16, 1999, to a year in jail and ordered to pay restitution of $41,735.

Appeal: Appeal to the Saskatchewan Court of Appeal heard on January 18, 2000. A two-to-one split decision upholding the conviction was announced on April 28, 2000. An appeal before the Supreme Court of Canada is pending.

✣ ✣ ✣

Name: Beattie Martin

Position(s) held: MLA for Regina Wascana and cabinet minister.

Charge: Charged in January 1997 with one count of fraud over $5,000. Accused of submitting false expense claims to get $23,410 from his Communication Allowance.

Preliminary hearing: Commenced on August 18, 1997.

Pleaded guilty: Pleaded guilty on March 11, 1999, of receiving $2,900 through false expense claims; Court of Queen's Bench Justice Catherine Dawson presiding; Crown prosecutor, Sharon Pratchler; defence lawyer, Aaron Fox.

Sentence: Granted a conditional discharge, placed on probation for a year, and ordered to perform 200 hours of community service. He repaid the $2,900.

✣ ✣ ✣